THE
URSULINE
SISTERS
of
Youngstown

THE
URSULINE
SISTERS
of
Youngstown

SERVING THE
MAHONING VALLEY
SINCE 1874

THOMAS WELSH

Michele Ristich Gatts,

Contributing Editor

FOREWORD BY ED O'NEILL

THE
History
PRESS

Published by The History Press
Charleston, SC
www.historypress.com

First published 2024
Updated 2024

Manufactured in the United States

ISBN 9781467156547

Library of Congress Control Number: 2023949136

Notice: The information in this book is true and complete to the best of our knowledge. It is offered without guarantee on the part of the author or The History Press. The author and The History Press disclaim all liability in connection with the use of this book.

Strive to be faithful to that which God has called you.
—Saint Angela Merici

CONTENTS

FOREWORD

The first time I saw a nun was when my mother took me to first grade at Saint Edward's Elementary School on Youngstown's north side. My teacher was Sister Rosemary. I think I was afraid. I was six years old and had never seen a nun. In those days, they wore the habit. From that day until I graduated from high school, I learned that the nuns were the backbone of the whole enterprise. In the same way that a family needs a mother to operate at full strength, you couldn't have a proper Catholic school without the nuns. Their dedication to teaching in general was unmatched.

Hollywood actor Ed O'Neill poses with Sister Mary Alyce Koval at Beatitude House during a 2013 fundraising campaign for the nonprofit organization. *Courtesy of Ursuline Sisters of Youngstown.*

Since those days in the '50s and early '60s, challenges in numbers have pushed the Ursuline Sisters to evolve, to take on other areas of service, providing care for the sick and shelter for the homeless. Their contributions to the Youngstown area cannot be measured, and it is time these remarkable women are recognized and appreciated for their selfless dedication and tireless efforts to help those in need. A fitting tribute would be to elect an Ursuline Sister as the next pope.

Ed O'Neill
Los Angeles, California
July 5, 2023

ACKNOWLEDGEMENTS

I would like to thank the many people who contributed their time, expertise and encouragement. This book would not exist without the support of Sister Mary McCormick, general superior of the Ursuline Sisters of Youngstown, who allocated critical resources, identified potential informants and reviewed the manuscript. At the same time, I owe a special debt of gratitude to Michele Ristich Gatts, whose superb communications work for the Ursuline Sisters of Youngstown simplified the task of finding a publisher and who has since cooperated with me on almost every aspect of this project. This historical narrative also benefited from the support of Sister Bridget Nolan, an archivist with the Ursuline Sisters of Youngstown; H. William Lawson, the executive director of the Mahoning Valley Historical Society; Pam Speis, an archivist with the Mahoning Valley Historical Society; Joan Reedy Lawson, the chancellor and archivist of the Catholic Diocese of Youngstown; Mark Brown, the former general manager of the Vindicator Printing Co.; Father Richard Murphy, the president of Ursuline High School; Carolyn Korenic, the director of alumni and advancement at Ursuline High School; Debbie DelQuadri, the secretary of Saint Patrick Church (Youngstown); and Bill Crawford, an archivist with Saint Patrick Church (Youngstown). As always, I received valuable assistance from the researchers at the Public Library of Youngstown and Mahoning County. Outside reviewers of the manuscript included Dr. Paul McBride, an emeritus professor of history at Ithaca College, and Benjamin J. Lariccia, the coauthor of *Coal War in the Mahoning Valley*. Ed O'Neill, an alumnus of Ursuline High School, also commented on the manuscript and graciously supplied the book's foreword. Throughout this journey, scores of individuals took time to share their memories and impressions. Interviewees ranged from past and present members of the Ursuline religious community to clerical leaders and former students of parish or diocesan schools. I benefited from the continuous encouragement of friends and relatives, including Jeannette Welsh, Anthony Dudzik, Robert Welsh, Sapna Welsh, Barbie DeLucia and Michael K. Geltz. I am especially grateful to my late mother, Elaine M. Welsh, who encouraged my early interest in writing and provided constant support. A longtime friend of the Ursuline Sisters of Youngstown, she was delighted to learn about this project, which materialized a few weeks before her passing in May 2022.

Thomas Welsh
Youngstown, Ohio
August 10, 2023

Introduction

"MEETING THE NEEDS
OF THE TIMES"

O n the afternoon of Wednesday, December 11, 1963, the sisters, novices and postulants of Youngstown, Ohio's Ursuline religious community relocated to their new motherhouse, a $1.2 million complex in the neighboring suburb of Canfield. At the time of the move, area residents were still reeling from the death of U.S. president John F. Kennedy, who had been assassinated in Dallas nineteen days earlier.

A welcome distraction came the following Sunday, when the *Youngstown Vindicator*, the metropolitan area's largest newspaper, placed a story about the Ursulines' move on the front page of its features section. Readers were informed that the modern, two-story structure could "accommodate 115 nuns and students," many of whom were being relocated from two older facilities: a nineteenth-century brick convent just north of downtown Youngstown and the former motherhouse, a mansion in Liberty Township that once served as the residence of an industrialist.[1]

The construction project, launched two years earlier with a well-publicized fundraising campaign, was presented as a milestone in the religious community's lengthy history. Media reports indicated that the Ursulines' roots in the Youngstown area could be traced back to 1874, when six nuns arrived from nearby Cleveland to staff a school connected to Saint Columba's Church, the city's premier Roman Catholic parish. From these humble beginnings, the community grew exponentially.

By the early 1960s, the Ursuline Sisters of Youngstown were a veritable force within the Mahoning Valley, commanding the attention and respect of the entire metropolitan area. Indeed, their purchase of the 130-acre site in Canfield was facilitated by an advisory committee that included some of the region's most prominent business leaders and professionals.[2]

Within less than a year, on May 24, 1964, the new facility was dedicated by the Most Reverend Emmet M. Walsh, the bishop of Youngstown. The ceremony was preceded by a series of crowded open house events. One local newspaper reported that "16,000 persons fought their way through a traffic jam to visit the nuns' new motherhouse, and other thousands were frustrated by the same traffic jam." The news article noted that the facility's "airy, bright" rooms and elegant chapel "give the Ursulines reasons for being tempted to the un-sisterly sin of pride."[3]

From all appearances, the Ursuline Sisters had embarked on an exciting new chapter of their journey, one likely to involve a continuous expansion of their numbers and infrastructure. Developments of the previous decade were encouraging. Ten years earlier, in 1954, Ursuline High School, an institution the religious community founded in 1905, was expanded under diocesan control. That same year, Bishop Walsh had dedicated the new physical plant of Cardinal Mooney High School, a move that reflected his optimism about the future of the Diocese of Youngstown.

Statistics appeared to support this high level of confidence. In 1959, parish enrollment in Youngstown and surrounding Mahoning County reached an all-time high, with 16,914 students on the rolls.[4] Two years later, in 1961, a Youngstown School Board estimate indicated that 13,318 students were enrolled in Catholic schools—elementary and secondary—while 27,324 attended public schools. In short, about one-third of the city's school-age population was enrolled in Catholic schools.[5]

In the six decades since the completion of the Ursuline Motherhouse, however, the religious community has been thoroughly transformed, along with the surrounding metropolitan area. Built in the early 1960s to accommodate more than one hundred residents, the motherhouse today serves fewer than thirty nuns, while the onetime industrial center of Youngstown, whose population peaked at 170,000, hosts fewer than 40,000 residents.

That said, the story of the Ursuline Sisters of Youngstown is hardly a narrative of entropy and decline. Like scores of religious communities throughout the northeastern United States, the Ursulines have struggled to address difficulties arising from declining vocations, ideological divisions, deindustrialization, depopulation and chronic economic inequality.

In response to these challenges, they have drawn on the example of their founder, Saint Angela Merici, who envisioned members of her order

Sister Patricia
McNicholas (*left*) and
Sister Carole Suhar
review a nineteenth-
century ledger at the
community's archives.
*Courtesy of Ursuline
Sisters of Youngstown.*

as beacons of Christian values who would assist in the revitalization of a weakened and compromised church.

Widely seen as a force for good within the larger community, the Ursuline Sisters of Youngstown have engaged in outreach to the poor involving strategic partnerships with members of the laity. Although they have earned wide respect for their contributions as classroom educators, today's Ursulines take no less pride in ministries that benefit those at the margins of society.

Significantly, the religious community's programs for single mothers, including Beatitude House, call to mind Saint Angela's determination to assist women who had been exploited by the military occupiers of Brescia in sixteenth-century Italy. In the same vein, the Ursulines' work with those affected by HIV/AIDS echoes Saint Angela's celebrated compassion for those suffering from syphilis, who were then stigmatized and denied admission to conventional hospitals.

The order's present-day leaders discern striking parallels between the challenges Saint Angela faced and those confronting contemporary American Catholics. Now, as in her time, shrinking numbers of clergy and religious people highlight a need for meaningful lay participation in a divided church. Hence, the Ursuline Sisters' efforts to address the needs of the present have brought them closer than ever to their spiritual foundations.

FORMING A RELIGIOUS COMMUNITY

On the morning of September 18, 1874, six Ursuline Sisters from Cleveland arrived in the bustling industrial city of Youngstown, Ohio. At precisely 11:00 a.m., they were met at downtown's Erie Terminal by Father Patrick H. Brown, the pastor of Youngstown's Saint Columba Church, who had invited the Ursuline nuns to staff his parish's elementary school. Father Brown, a stout, balding man known for his cheerful disposition, was already showing symptoms of the progressive "paralysis" that would claim his life four years later.[6]

The ailing pastor was presumably friendly and attentive to Mother Mary Theresa Foley, the superior of the small religious community. His warmest words, however, were likely reserved for his sibling, Sister Angela Brown, whose presence in the Cleveland Ursuline community directly influenced his decision to obtain their services.

The remaining members of the cohort—Sister Ursula Croxton, Sister Saint John Radnor, Sister Felix Polion and Sister Saint James Sullivan— would go on to dedicate themselves to the project of Catholic education in the Youngstown area. Yet their first glimpse of the mill town must have given them pause.

As they left the railway station, the nuns encountered a downtown retail district studded with handsome brick and stone buildings, but their eyes were drawn invariably to the dense pall of reddish fumes that hung over the community like a canopy—evidence of its expanding iron sector.

This photograph shows the southwest corner of Youngstown's Central Square in about 1870. *Courtesy of Mahoning Valley Historical Society.*

Looking out on this smoke-filled vista, Mother Mary Theresa may have experienced a premonition of the difficult months that lay ahead. The mother superior was almost certainly aware of the ethnic rivalries that bedeviled Youngstown's mostly working-class Catholic community. While the city was not yet the multiethnic "boomtown" it would become in the next few decades, Youngstown's overwhelmingly Northern European Catholics sparred over issues ranging from culture and language to liturgy and church politics.

In this regard, the local Catholic community resembled its larger counterpart in Cleveland, where German and Irish American factions were locked in a bitter struggle for political and cultural dominance. "From almost the year of its foundation as a diocese in 1847, Cleveland was beset by two factions, one composed of ethnically self-conscious Irish clerics and laymen and the other of Germans, whose ethnic jealousies found expression in a multitude of issues and controversies," Henry B. Leonard observed in his monograph on the ethnic tensions that shaped the early twentieth-century American church.[7]

The Ursuline nuns who arrived that late summer morning in 1874 were well acquainted with the controversies plaguing the Diocese of Cleveland, which then included Youngstown. Several of the sisters were reportedly outspoken critics of former Cleveland bishop Louis Amadeus Rappe, who had resigned four years earlier in 1870 amid widespread criticism and rumors of failing health.

Since his appointment as the first bishop of Cleveland in 1847, the French-born episcopal leader had struggled to establish a reputation for impartiality. Nevertheless, Bishop Rappe became a polarizing figure, as many of the diocese's Irish American clerics regarded his policies as preferential to German American Catholics.

While commonplace ethnocentricity played a role in this conflict, it was also true that the issues dividing the two groups were substantial. German Catholics, for example, favored a model of the American church in which parishes functioned as reservoirs of language and culture, while the Irish promoted neighborhood, or "territorial," parishes that privileged religious identity over ethnic identity.[8]

By the time the Ursulines arrived in Youngstown, the Diocese of Cleveland was under the steady leadership of Bishop Richard Gilmour, a Scottish-born convert to Roman Catholicism. As it turned out, Bishop Gilmour showed little patience for political infighting that stemmed from ethnic rivalry. His policy of zero tolerance, as we might describe it today, would eventually threaten the existence of Youngstown's Ursuline community, which seemingly exemplified the sort of ethnic tension the bishop found so distasteful.

This critical juncture, however, was more than a couple of years away. For the time being, the Ursuline nuns who settled in Youngstown found much to occupy their attention and were able to temporarily put aside political differences that were evidently encouraged by their community of origin in Cleveland.

Upon their arrival at the parish complex, the travel-weary nuns were invited to dine with Father Brown at the rectory of Saint Columba Church. Afterward, they retired to a small frame building that had been prepared for them near the corner of Elm Street and West Rayen Avenue, a block northwest of the church's towering edifice.

Their convent abutted a large, brick, three-story school building that had been completed three years earlier in 1871. The industrious nuns wasted no

The second edifice of Saint Columba Parish stood at the intersection of Wood and Elm Streets. *Courtesy of Mahoning Valley Historical Society.*

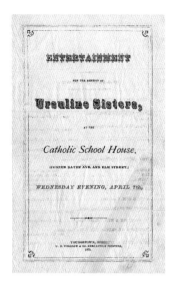

ENTERTAINMENT

FOR THE BENEFIT OF

Ursuline Sisters,

AT THE

Catholic School House,

(CORNER BAYEN AVE. AND ELM STREET.)

WEDNESDAY EVENING, APRIL 7th,

YOUNGSTOWN, OHIO.
U. S. WORDON & CO. NEWCASTLE PRINTERS,
1875.

This 1875 program was distributed at a fundraiser to benefit the Ursuline Sisters' schoolhouse. *Courtesy of Ursuline Sisters of Youngstown.*

time putting it to use. Within four days of their arrival, they opened classes for sixty girls, while the lay teachers who had previously staffed the school concentrated on the instruction of boys. If this arrangement was consistent with the order's traditions, the school's male students made it clear they wished to be taught by the nuns as well.

Over the next few years, these boys became more insistent in their demands, and by the late 1870s, ninety of them had "formed an army of protest." To avoid further mischief, the pastor finally requested the services of a teaching nun to address the boys' educational needs.[9]

There is no evidence, however, that similar outbreaks of student resistance occurred during the early 1870s, and the general atmosphere at Saint Columba School was subdued. Sister Felix briskly expanded the community's educational outreach by opening a class for twenty-five students in the convent's largest room. Likewise, Sister Angela made good use of a piano donated by her brother, Father Brown, when she moved it to the convent's parlor and began to teach music lessons.

Remarkably, on September 24, just six days after the nuns' arrival in Youngstown, the religious community began work on an addition to the convent. The new addition, comprising two spacious classrooms, was completed on November 18, 1874.[10] Less than a year later, on April 7, 1875, the Ursulines held a benefit at the school building, where students participated in skits and musical numbers.[11]

Yet the religious community, for all its accomplishments, was eventually crippled by political discord. The details of these disagreements have been lost to history, but they evidently arose from the ethnic rivalry that flourished in every sector of the American church.

In 1878, the disturbing situation in Youngstown caught the attention of Bishop Gilmour himself, who scheduled a personal visit to the convent. By then, Sister Mary Therese, worn down by the infighting, had resigned her position as superior. She was replaced, in 1875, by Mother Louis Malin, who benefited from the assistance of Mother Saint Joseph Steiner and Sister Ann of Jesus Madden.

Despite the three women's combined efforts, however, the conflict continued. "The taint of nationalism unfortunately affected the first group of Ursulines to take up residence in Youngstown—the same evil which brought about the resignation of Bishop Rappe," explained Sister Lelia Mahoney, Order of Saint Ursula (OSU), in her narrative history of the Ursuline Sisters of Toledo, Ohio. Compounding the situation was the fact that some members of the religious community "had relatives among the priests" who became entangled in the controversy, inspiring "sympathy and prejudice for or against" the opposing sides.

Once Bishop Gilmour was forced to intervene, he had no desire to mince words. During a face-to-face meeting with the sisters, the bishop announced that the religious community would be disbanded. Given Bishop Gilmour's reputation for tough-mindedness, few observers could have predicted what happened next. Sister Felix, one of the community's six original members, approached the bishop and initiated an intervention of her own:

> When [Bishop Gilmour] *was about to leave, Sr. Felix Polion, while conducting him to the gate, asked him to reconsider. Surprised, he told her that only infrequently did he change his mind. "Your Lordship," she said, "even God Himself changed his mind." Astonished, the Bishop asked her for an instance. She replied, "God warned the people of Ninevah He would destroy their city in forty days. They repented and did penance[,] and He forgave them."*

This challenge evidently caught Bishop Gilmour off guard, and he signaled that he was open to suggestions. At that point, Sister Felix urged the prelate to consider placing the community under the leadership of a superior from the Ursuline community in Toledo, which "had never been involved in the controversy over ethnic supremacy." To the surprise of everyone on hand, the bishop reentered the convent and "put the proposition before the nuns."[12]

A short time later, on July 22, 1878, Mother Lawrence McCaffrey of Toledo was appointed as superior of the fledgling community, an event that contributed to a long period of stability and development. Mother Lawrence was accompanied by a small group of teaching nuns, and yet another cohort arrived from Toledo in late August that year, "satisfying not only the wants of St. Columba's school, but also those of St. Joseph's," a neighboring institution connected to a German American parish.[13]

The tumultuous beginnings of the Ursuline religious community in Youngstown must be understood within the larger context of the late

Mother Lawrence McCaffrey led the community through a period of expansive development. *Courtesy of Ursuline Sisters of Youngstown.*

nineteenth century, a period in which the Roman Catholic Church found itself in a state of flux. The First Vatican Council, opened by Pius IX in June 1868, was speedily adjourned in October 1870, when the Italian army captured Rome, marking the final defeat of the Papal States and ushering in the unification of the Italian Peninsula. By then, the council had approved two constitutions that reflected the church's growing concerns about modern ideologies—including nationalism—that seemed irreconcilable with its own institutional values.

The most controversial of these documents was the First Dogmatic Constitution on the Church of Christ (*Pastor aeternus*), which enshrined the primacy and infallibility of the pope.[14] Even some of those Catholic leaders who agreed with the spirit of the constitution questioned its timing, and their fears were seemingly validated when *Pastor aeternus* inspired a new wave of anti-Catholic sentiment within the country's Protestant establishment, which already harbored suspicions that Rome's influence would undermine American democratic values.

Despite these troubling developments, the Ursuline Sisters who arrived in Youngstown in 1874 were probably more inclined to focus on signs of continuity than consider the untold ways in which historical forces had shaped their church. For that matter, the formative years of their own religious community had become shrouded in mystery.

Few Ursuline Sisters, for instance, had a plain understanding of the order's beginnings as a loosely organized community of laywomen in sixteenth-century Brescia, Italy. They certainly venerated the memory of their founder, Angela Merici, who had been canonized as a saint in the Catholic Church sixty-seven years earlier. Yet it is unclear how knowledgeable many of them were about the personal struggles and external conditions that informed Angela's decision to organize the Company of Saint Ursula in a once-prosperous Italian city laid to waste by foreign invaders.

The sisters presumably internalized the broad outlines of their origin story. They would have known, for instance, that on November 25, 1535, the company's twelve original members—joined by fifteen others later that day—had consecrated themselves to the service of God on the Feast Day of

Saint Catherine of Alexandria, a legendary martyr who is said to have died at the hands of a Roman emperor.

It was also common knowledge that Angela Merici placed the small community under the patronage of Saint Ursula, another legendary martyr. Less familiar, perhaps, were the details of the long, complicated journey that brought the Ursulines to their prevailing status as a cloistered religious community admired for its commitment to formal education.

Origins of a Religious Community

The story of Angela Merici is probably greater than the sum of its parts—and researchers' understanding of her life and times is hardly complete. Born in the early 1470s in the city of Desenzano on the southwestern shore of Lake Garda, Angela apparently enjoyed an idyllic early childhood. Her father was a farmer in the Desenzano district who migrated from the neighboring town of Brescia, where Angela spent her most active years. Her mother, on the other hand, belonged to the Biancosi family, members of the lesser nobility in the nearby town of Salò.

Angela's biographer, Sister Teresa Ledochowska, OSU, explained that during this time, "marriages between members of different social ranks caused no surprise."[15] Still, this aspect of her birth sheds light on the ease with which Angela moved among people of different backgrounds—a quality central to the effectiveness of her ministry.[16]

According to most accounts of her life, Angela was orphaned at the age of ten and, along with her sister, taken in by an uncle who lived in Salò. As a teenager, she was overwhelmed by the death of her sister, with whom she had enjoyed a close relationship.

Shortly thereafter, Angela experienced a vision in which "she saw heaven open and a glorious procession of angels and virgins advancing two by two." One of the virgins, whom she recognized as her deceased sister, "told Angela that God wanted to make use of her to found a Company of consecrated virgins…that…would grow rapidly."[17]

During her years in Salò, Angela joined the Third Order of the Franciscans of Strict Observance, introduced by Saint Francis of Assisi "to enable the laity to devote themselves to the service of the Church."[18] Her entrance into the tertiary order "brought her into a tide of spiritual energy which flowed into apostolic work."[19]

There are few reliable accounts of Angela's activities during the period that elapsed between her entrance into the Third Order of Franciscans and her arrival in Brescia in 1516, but much is known about the era's political, military and religious upheavals.

At the heart of the region's difficulties was a senseless war. In 1494, Ludovico Il Moro, the duke of Milan, sought the assistance of French troops during a territorial dispute with the King of Naples. When French monarch Charles VIII ordered a full-scale invasion of Northern Italy, the people of Brescia initially welcomed their French occupiers, but they soon became disillusioned.

For one thing, the presence of soldiers within the city contributed to a steep rise in venereal disease, especially syphilis, which Italians called "the French illness."[20] For another, citizens became enraged over their French occupiers' efforts to impose a rigid class system—one that stood in sharp contrast to the fluid society that prevailed beforehand.

In 1511, the people of Brescia rose to expel their oppressors. The French, in retaking the city, engaged in massacres, the wholesale destruction of property and widespread looting. As Sister Teresa observed, "Not only Italy, but all Europe was stunned by the enormity of the disaster."[21]

Almost forty years old when she arrived in Brescia, Angela was determined to make a positive difference. She forged close ties with members of a secret male lay organization known as the Company of the Divino Amore, whose activities centered on the organization of a hospital for "incurables" (i.e., those suffering from syphilis). One member recalled, "[Angela] spoke to me with such loving kindness that she made me her captive, so to speak."[22]

He was not alone in his reverence for "Madre Angela." Scores of testimonials attest to her ability to influence others in the pursuit of "apostolic" efforts focusing on the poor and marginalized. Evidence suggests that one group of women under Angela's influence was involved in the care of men afflicted with syphilis.

Yet those suffering from the "incurable" disease were not the only casualties of Brescia's foreign occupation who benefited from Angela's sympathetic attention. "The most disturbing social problem was the growth of a young generation both insolent and vicious, emancipated from all the restraints of discipline," Sister Teresa observed. "Orphans, robbed of their parents by war and disease, found themselves thrown on the streets, surrounded by perils, and victims of vice from their childhood." Under such extreme conditions, the challenge "of protecting and educating young girls became one of acute urgency."[23]

While Angela was based in Brescia, she traveled extensively, despite the region's turbulent political climate. Even her residence in Brescia left her vulnerable to the prospect of violence. Nevertheless, between 1520 and 1529, she participated in pilgrimages to the neighboring city of Mantua, the Holy Land, Rome and Sacro Monti di Varallo ("the Sacred Mountain of Varallo"), a devotional complex featuring an imaginative recreation of Jerusalem.[24]

During her stay in Rome, Angela enjoyed a private audience with Pope Clement VII, who was aware of her work with the Company of the Divino Amore to establish hospitals for "incurables." When the pope urged her to remain in Rome to work in the city's Centre for Charities, "Angela deferentially made her excuses" and departed for Brescia—a bold move for anyone of that period, especially a woman.[25]

An atmosphere of relative calm returned to Northern Italy in 1530, when Charles V, the Holy Roman emperor, signed a peace treaty with the Republic of Venice, ending a period of almost continual strife. With hundreds of other Brescians, Angela trudged back to the beleaguered city from a temporary refuge in nearby Cremona. She was, by then, almost sixty years old, but she was determined to lay the groundwork for what became the Company of Saint Ursula.

Shortly after the new organization's rule won ecclesiastical approval, elections were held, and Angela emerged as "Mother, Mistress, and Treasurer for the term of her life."[26] Far from a micromanager, Angela envisioned her company as one that would strive to meet the needs of the times, and she made allowances for changes in its rule if deemed necessary.

At the same time, the eclectic nature of the community reflected Angela's unique ability to bring together people of divergent backgrounds—a quality conveyed in the Italian maxim *Siate piazzevole* ("Be like a piazza"). As Sister Martha Buser, OSU, explained, "A piazza is open[,] and it knows people are going to come in and people are going to go out, but it is always going to stay open."[27]

Following Angela's death in 1540, five years after she organized the Company of Saint Ursula, the religious community spread throughout Brescia. Twenty-five years later, in 1565, the first community outside of Brescia was established in the town of Cremona, also in the region of Lombardy.

A year later, in 1566, Saint Charles Borromeo, the archbishop of the Lombardian capital of Milan, paved the way for the community's foundation in that city while making significant modifications in its rule. Concerned about the vulnerability of women living independently, Charles urged them to form a community. However, the archbishop's recommendations also

This pastel drawing of Saint Angela Merici by nineteenth-century Italian artist Pietro Calzavacca shows her instructing a young woman. *Courtesy of Merician Museum, Brescia, Italy.*

reflected his role as a promulgator of the reforms of the Council of Trent, which encouraged stricter rules for religious communities.

By the early 1600s, Ursuline foundations were located throughout Italy and had spread to other parts of Europe, including France. In 1610,

Madame de Sainte-Beauve, the influential widow of a French jurist, invited a group of Ursulines led by Mother Frances de Bermond to establish a Parisian community.

Under the leadership of Mother Frances, the community was transformed into a monastery of cloistered nuns, and their vows were amended to include a formal commitment to education. This "fourth vow" became central to the community's identity, as the French Ursulines were determined, despite their cloistered status, "to preserve and foster the original apostolic thrust that Angela had given them."[28]

From Paris, Ursuline communities were established in Amiens and Abbeville, and these gave rise to a new foundation in Boulogne-sur-Mer, organized on August 27, 1624. More than two centuries later, this community played a role in the establishment of the first Ursuline community in Northeast Ohio, with Louis Amadeus Rappe, the future bishop of Cleveland, serving as a major catalyst. In the late 1830s, when Father Rappe acted as the chaplain of the Ursulines in Boulogne-sur-Mer, "he was inspired to serve as a missionary in America."

The priest kept the Ursulines in mind in 1847, when he was appointed the episcopal leader of the new Diocese of Cleveland. Three years later, in 1850, Bishop Rappe "requested, and after much persuasion, secured a band of Ursulines for Cleveland…with Mother Mary of the Annunciation as the first superior."[29]

For all the twists and turns in the history of the Ursuline Sisters, one can trace a relatively direct line between the Company of Saint Ursula, the organization founded by Saint Angela Merici in 1535, and the small community established in Youngstown during the late summer of 1874.

Yet in some respects, the two communities could not have been more different. Over time, the heirs to Saint Angela's spiritual gift, or "charism," have found it necessary to reinvent themselves to meet new challenges, and the Ursuline Sisters of Youngstown would prove no exception to this pattern.

BUILDING AN INFRASTRUCTURE

With Mother Lawrence McCaffrey at the helm of Youngstown's Ursuline community, the sisters set out to shore up their local presence. Endowed with a "keen intellect and kindly, peaceable and charitable nature," Mother Lawrence proved to be an effective administrator.[30] Moreover, her openness to collaboration enabled her to establish a cooperative relationship with the church's new pastor.

After the untimely death of Father Brown in 1878, Irish-born Father Edward Mears assumed the pastorate of Saint Columba Parish and quickly earned a reputation as a man of vision. One year later, in 1879, Mother Lawrence came to Father Mears with a proposal. The superior offered to purchase the property her community occupied, which they were then renting from Father Mears. A deal was struck, and Mother Lawrence agreed to make regular $100 payments on the $6,000 debt for the property—a promise she apparently kept.

Records indicate that between October 1879 and December 1881, the Ursulines reduced their debt to $3,200. Father Mears, in turn, offered to donate the balance to the Ursulines and retire the debt. By the spring of 1882, Mother Lawrence had the community incorporated under the title Ursuline Academy of the Holy Name of Jesus, which highlighted its educational purpose. Yet the decision had other long-term benefits, as incorporating "enables its members to act as a unit, undisturbed by change of members, and it continues as long as the corporation endures."[31]

In the late nineteenth century, the Ursuline religious community was closely identified with Saint Columba School, whose brick and stone edifice towered above the sisters' frame convent with its quaint picket fence. The school, located a block north of Saint Columba Church, would emerge as a center of local Catholic life, with an educational program that was expanded to include secondary-level classes.

Connected to Youngstown's premier Catholic parish, the institution had experienced steady growth since 1860, when it occupied a small frame building at the corner of Hazel and Wood Streets. The original school stood across from the first wooden edifice of Saint Columba Church, an institution organized by Irish immigrants in 1847.

In 1870, just two years after the completion of the parish's second edifice, then-pastor Father Eugene O'Callaghan purchased land on the southwest corner of Elm Street and West Rayen Avenue. On that spot, in 1871, Father O'Callaghan oversaw the construction of a three-story building in the Romanesque Revival style.

During its first years of operation, the school benefited from the presence of Immaculate Heart of Mary nuns from Cleveland, who had been teaching at the parish since 1860. There is no question, though, that the arrival of the Ursulines in 1874 constituted a new chapter in the institution's history.

The second edifice of Saint Columba School stood on the southwest corner of Elm Street and West Rayen Avenue. *Courtesy of Mahoning Valley Historical Society.*

By the 1890s, the parish school was one of the community's most visible institutions. Its commencement exercises were social events with elaborate theatrical productions.[32] Over time, Saint Columba School would claim its share of prominent alumni, including Edward Mooney, the future archbishop of Detroit.

Yet even as the Ursulines' reputation as educators grew, they discovered that their services were not always considered sufficient by pastors of national parishes, which were often committed to preserving the language and culture of specific ethnic communities. For the most part, the Ursuline Sisters found their earliest opportunities among the community's territorial parishes, also referred to as "English-speaking parishes."

On February 12, 1883, four Ursuline nuns opened the parish school at Immaculate Conception Church, which had been organized on the city's east side one year earlier. During its first year of operation, the institution occupied a portion of the church's original wooden edifice. Seating was tight, and one local newspaper reported "there were about 175 boys and girls enrolled" at a school that took up the church's first floor and a segment of the chapel.

Eight years later, a new church was built, and the rooms of the older frame building were used as classrooms. A steady increase in enrollment, however, guaranteed that overcrowding would remain a problem, and the parish school was forced to seek space in nearby buildings, including the church itself.[33]

By modern standards, the small frame school was overcrowded and understaffed. One alumnus later recalled, "We were a hundred strong in the old classroom—50 to a side of the old-time pot-bellied stove."[34] Yet the school, for all its physical limitations, was a locus of community activity and source of neighborhood pride.

Its staff—which included Scottish-born Mother Columba Gettins (the principal), three teaching nuns and two lay teachers—encouraged high levels of student involvement in local, regional and national events. In 1893, for example, its students assembled a prize-winning exhibit of their schoolwork for the Chicago World's Fair.[35]

In 1888, five years after the establishment of Immaculate Conception School, three Ursuline nuns were sent to reopen the school at Saint Ann's Church in the incorporated village of Brier Hill. According to a program commemorating the parish's seventy-fifth anniversary on October 29, 1944, the school had been established in 1872 and was originally staffed by the Sisters of the Humility of Mary. When the Ursulines reopened the institution in 1888, Saint Ann School benefited from the work of such educators as Mother Bernard McCann and Mother Norbert Reilly.[36]

That same year, two Ursuline nuns opened a subsidiary to Saint Columba School on Franklin Avenue in a southside neighborhood known as "Kilkenny." Six years later, in 1894, the school's two locations reportedly served a total of 994 students. (Other milestones of the period included the construction of the Ursuline convent's more than $2,000 chapel in 1885.)

Mother Lawrence's plans to expand the Ursulines' reach didn't stop there. Between 1888 and 1889, the community purchased two lots and houses adjoining their property for $2,500 and $4,000, respectively. The rental of these properties over the next decade "added nearly $20,000 annually to the community's income."[37]

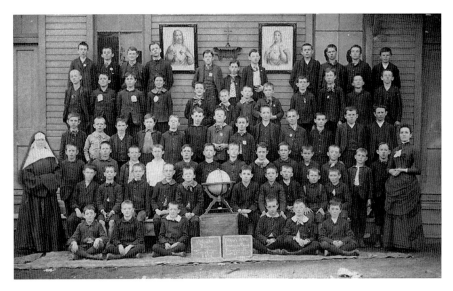

In September 1888, male students at Immaculate Conception School benefited from a teaching staff that included Sister Mary Margaret McCabe (*left*). *Courtesy of Ursuline Sisters of Youngstown.*

These developments overlapped with an era of explosive growth that was manifested in the transformation of Saint Columba Parish. In 1896, not long after Father Mears began work on the splendid neo-Gothic structure that would replace the second brick edifice of Saint Columba Church, Mother Lawrence announced plans to build a new convent on the site of the existing one, which sat west of the parish school on the corner of Elm Street and West Rayen Avenue.

By that time, the local Ursuline community, with thirty-six members, had outgrown the small frame building that had served its needs since 1874.

To initiate the project, Mother Lawrence sent an application to Cleveland bishop Ignatius Frederick Horstmann, who succeeded Bishop Gilmour following his death in 1891. The superior's letter to Bishop Horstmann indicated it would cost $30,000 to build the new convent, which was envisioned to rise four stories and stretch 115 feet along West Rayen Avenue.

Fundraising was critical to the plan's realization, as Mother Lawrence listed the community's assets as $8,000 in cash, along with $12,000 in overdue compensation for teaching services to the city's parish schools. As Ursuline chroniclers Sister Anne Lynch and Sister Mary Ellen Dean observed, the latter figure "is evidence of the community's role in the recent depression," given that the nuns taught in the schools "even when they were not paid."

Left: Father Edward Mears, the pastor of Saint Columba Church, formed a cooperative relationship with Mother Lawrence McCaffrey. *Courtesy of Ursuline Sisters of Youngstown.*

Below: The four-story Ursuline convent once dominated the corner of West Rayen Avenue and Elm Street. *Courtesy of Ursuline Sisters of Youngstown.*

Once Bishop Horstmann approved the application, work on the convent began promptly. A groundbreaking ceremony was held on May 18, 1896, with "Mother Lawrence herself turning the first sod," and the building's cornerstone was laid on June 30 that same year.[38] Remarkably, the Ursuline Sisters moved into their new home in February 1897.

It is difficult today to imagine how Mother Lawrence's convent once dominated the block of West Rayen Avenue, located just west of Elm Street. Its former site currently hosts a small commercial building that adjoins a parking lot. In the winter of 1897, however, the new convent captivated a reporter at the London-based *Catholic Universe*, whose detailed description of the building was reprinted in both of Youngstown's major newspapers.

Hailing the new landmark as a "splendid edifice," the *Universe* went on to praise its "plain and unassuming" style. "The building…presents a square front to [West Rayen Avenue] and inclines…to the Ionic model of architecture," the reporter wrote. "A portico, flanked on either side by Ionic pillars, leads to the main entrance whose massive doors are of quartered oak." This entrance opened into "a tiled vestibule terminating in great swinging doors," beyond which could be found "an office austerely furnished" and "the first of three moderately sized reception rooms."

Meanwhile, the "convent proper" included "three inviting classrooms," along with "a refectory…with an adjoining pantry and kitchen replete with shelves and lockers of the newest pattern and finish." Those who ascended the staircase leading to the second floor encountered "a handsome window of art glass, cheerful in design and color."

The convent's second floor featured classrooms, music rooms and a library "well lighted by the side windows," while the third was "divided into sleeping apartments, three of the largest being devoted to the infirmary, so situated as to receive the morning sun." The fourth floor comprised "three…large apartments used as dormitories."

The building's artistic elements included "a solitary window of antique glass" with a "tastefully figured…representation of St. Angela teaching." Looking out on the busy thoroughfare of West Rayen Avenue, the window radiated the community's all-embracing commitment to education.[39]

Yet the convent, taken as a whole, sent another message—but one no less significant. While other religious orders staffed the institutions of Youngstown's growing Catholic community, the Ursuline Sisters alone had established a local presence. It was clear to area residents that the daughters of Saint Angela Merici were here to stay.

2

BUILDING ON A TRADITION OF EDUCATION

By the mid-1900s, a Youngstown native returning to the community after an extended absence would have been surprised at the dramatic improvements to its infrastructure. By then, the city's formerly isolated south side was linked to the downtown by the Market Street Viaduct, a 1,200-foot-long steel arch bridge spanning the Mahoning River, the valley's main waterway. At the heart of the metropolitan area sat Mill Creek Park, a wooded urban "playground" whose attractions included Lake Glacier, a forty-three-acre man-made body of water that enhanced "the beauty of the park's most northern reaches."[40]

These upgrades reflected, in turn, the transformation of the community's industrial base, which had focused on iron and coal production throughout the nineteenth century. In 1900, however, local industrialists George D. Wick and James A. Campbell organized the Youngstown Iron, Sheet and Tube Company (later known as Youngstown Sheet and Tube Company), which emerged as one of the country's most important regional steel producers.[41]

Naturally, the rise of the local steel industry had an impact on the city's population, which rose from 33,220 to 44,885 between 1890 and 1900—an increase of more than 11,000. Moreover, the population was on track to exceed 100,000 within a couple of decades.[42]

Nowhere was the city's development more evident than in the short block of Elm Street that ran north from Wood Street to West Rayen Avenue. At that time, the second edifice of Saint Columba Church was still standing at the southern end of Elm Street, although it served as the parish school's gymnasium.

The third edifice of Saint Columba Parish once towered above the city's downtown. *Courtesy of Mahoning Valley Historical Society.*

Deconsecrated after a final mass held in June 1903, the modest brick structure had given way to the parish's third edifice: a huge granite neo-Gothic structure with square towers that straddled a rose window glazed with stained glass. "The new church boasted 1,500 light bulbs outlining the Gothic arches and a floodlit sanctuary," one retrospective account observed. "There was an 18-foot-wide altar of unblemished Carrara marble, a statue of St. Columba in the carved screen behind the tabernacle, a 26-pipe organ, a large baptismal font…and a marble tablet on the wall listing donors."[43]

Farther up the block stood the three-story parish school called "the brick school" to distinguish it from the four-story convent school nearby.[44] This complex of institutions, which could be seen from the city's downtown retail district, represented the Catholic community's growing stature.

The expansion of the parish's infrastructure paralleled a steep rise in membership. By the late 1890s, Saint Columba Parish served about 600 families "representing some 2,000 souls." Many observers credited the leadership of Father Edward Mears, who had been named by the Diocese of Cleveland as the parish's "irremovable" pastor about a decade earlier. Since then, Father Mears had earned a reputation as a builder, given his involvement in the construction of the new church, the adjacent brick rectory and the new Ursuline convent up the street.[45]

The Ursuline nuns who staffed Saint Columba Parish School witnessed a similar expansion of their educational mission. In September 1905, for instance, the religious community opened Ursuline Academy, the forerunner of Ursuline High School. Under the leadership of Mother Joseph Hopkins, the superior, and Mother Vincent O'Connell, the principal, the Ursulines' "pay school" introduced grades nine through twelve for twenty-five female students, all of whom attended classes at the convent on West Rayen Avenue.

Despite the school's rather modest enrollment, it enjoyed a reputation for maintaining "high standards of spiritual values, social graces and academic achievement." This distinction owed much to the Ursulines' emphasis on the preparation of faculty. Prospective teachers generally attended the Ursuline Normal School and Sisters' College in Cleveland, but in special cases, teaching nuns were also permitted to attend other colleges and universities.[46]

On June 16, 1909, Father Mears presided over the Ursuline Academy's first commencement ceremony at Youngstown's Park Theater, where two students were singled out for honors: graduating seniors Eunice Marie Lawlor and Mary Agnes Maloney.[47]

Word of the high school's academic excellence spread, and by 1919, its student population had practically doubled. To address the issue of overcrowding at the convent school, the community purchased the former estate of industrialist Chauncey Andrews from his daughter, Mrs. John Logan.

Based in a once-exclusive neighborhood situated between Bryson Street and Wick Avenue on the city's north side, the estate hosted "a magnificent mansion with stained glass windows, inlaid floors, carved woodwork, and a beautifully designed stairway."

The luxurious edifice would serve as an overdue supplement to the convent on Rayen Avenue. Mother Bernard McCann, then serving as the school's principal, led the high school through a series of improvements. In 1922, for example, the institution became affiliated with the Catholic University of America in Washington, D.C.[48]

The Ursulines' establishment of their secondary school rounded out a period of almost uninterrupted achievement. By 1919, the religious community counted seventy members and provided teaching services to six parish schools, including Saint Columba, Saint Ann, Immaculate Conception, Saints Cyril and Methodius and Saints Peter and Paul, as well as Saint Rose in nearby Girard.[49]

While the Ursulines focused primarily on the needs of the local Catholic community, they won public admiration when they volunteered as nurses during the flu and pneumonia epidemic of 1918.[50]

Above: In April 1920, Mother Bernard McCann relaxed with students on the campus of Ursuline Academy. *Courtesy of Ursuline Sisters of Youngstown.*

Opposite: The edifice of what became Ursuline High School was completed in 1925, five years before it became a coeducational institution. *Courtesy of Ursuline High School.*

These far-ranging activities, however, did not detract from the Ursulines' progress in the realm of secondary education. The high school grew steadily, and in 1920, it was evident the institution had outgrown the Wick Avenue convent.

In response, Mother Joseph launched a community-wide fundraising effort for a new high school building, a campaign completed under her successor, Mother Agnes Ryan. Anticipating a steep rise in enrollment, the community's leadership envisioned a three-story building that would accommodate four hundred students.

Thanks to the assistance of prominent local citizens—including William Gillen, Charles Mooney, John Gerrity, Grant Whistler, Nellie McHugh and Sara Varley McCarthy—the project moved forward with breathtaking speed. A little more than a year after a groundbreaking ceremony took place on March 11, 1924, the new school building was completed.

Rising on a stretch of campus near Bryson Street, the buff brick-and-stone structure opened for classes in April 1925.[51] The teaching nuns who staffed the school resided at the former Chauncey Andrews Mansion, which sat northeast of the new building and looked toward Wick Avenue.[52] Slowly but surely, the once bucolic estate was taking on the appearance of a high school campus.

In 1927, two years after the building's completion, the high school was admitted to the North Central Association, a membership organization consisting of colleges, universities and schools in nineteen states engaged in educational accreditation.[53]

Even the Wall Street crash of 1929 and subsequent Great Depression failed to disrupt the school's progress. On the contrary, these developments evidently influenced Cleveland bishop Joseph Schrembs's decision to broaden the school's mission. In 1930, Bishop Schrembs, after expressing concern about the absence of Catholic secondary educational opportunities for boys in Greater Youngstown, recommended that the religious community turn the academy into a coed institution.

The Rise of Ursuline High School

At that point, Ursuline Academy became known officially as Ursuline High School. While this shift to coed status triggered a significant increase in enrollment, it also forced the religious community to relinquish a degree of control over an institution it had operated independently for a quarter century. "[When the Ursuline Sisters] accepted boys into the school, we also agreed to a priest as principal and a [male] coach," explained Sister Isabel Rudge. "That was not an easy decision."[54]

Fortunately, Father Edward Conry, after being tapped as the school's first male principal in 1930, proved to be "a very kind…priest," whose "gentle leadership…added much to the spirit of the school." The priest assumed administrative control over an institution that served 315 students, including 180 freshmen. Among other things, Father Conry oversaw an expansion of the curriculum, which would include "three foreign languages, English, three separate branches of history, a full complement of the physical sciences and mathematics, commercial, home economics and fine arts courses."

Physical education became a requirement for both boys and girls, while the school introduced basketball and football teams "for competition at the junior varsity level."[55] In 1934, the graduating class included the first boys who had attended Ursuline for four years. Significantly, this class, made up of thirty-eight boys and forty-five girls, included seven future Ursuline nuns: Sister Jerome Corcoran, Sister Anne Lynch, Sister Mary Catherine Doran, Sister Mary Conaboy, Sister Marie Hughes, Sister Victoria Pascarella and Sister Marie Denise Barnes.[56]

As the high school developed, the name Ursuline Academy became attached to a small elementary school that operated on the northwestern edge of campus. Sister Isabel Rudge, who attended Ursuline Academy in the late 1930s and mid-1940s, indicated that space at the elementary school was exceptionally tight.

The academy's first- and second-grade classes were combined, and several of the nuns taught multiple grade levels. Despite these limitations, the academy exposed its students to opportunities they might not have enjoyed otherwise, including the chance to meet children from other parts of the city.

Classes were originally held at the old estate's former carriage house—a structure later known as the "Arts Building." While the campus hosted several facilities, including the convent and the new three-story building, the secondary school was soon starved for space due to rising enrollment. "Then, Ursuline High School needed our building…so they decided to move the students from [the carriage house] down to [the convent on] West Rayen Avenue," Sister Isabel recalled.

When the school closed in the mid-1940s, many of its former students found themselves in unfamiliar parochial schools. However, Sister Isabel's

This 1930 photograph of Youngstown's downtown captures the vitality of a city with 170,000 residents. *Courtesy of Mahoning Valley Historical Society.*

transition was relatively smooth, as the Ursuline nuns also staffed Saint Columba School, where she completed her junior high coursework.

Sister Isabel recalled that her seventh-grade teacher, Sister Jerome Corcoran, taught her the "Irish jig" and also encouraged her to embrace Saint Columba School's ethnic and racial diversity. "Had I not known it was an 'Irish' parish, I don't think I would have figured it out," Sister Isabel noted. Over the next two years, she sang in the girls' choir and participated in church processions—experiences that fueled her lifelong love of liturgy.[57]

By the time the Ursuline Academy closed its doors, Ursuline High School was thriving under the leadership of Father Joseph Gallagher, who succeeded Father Conry as principal in 1938.[58] When Sister Isabel Rudge entered the school as a freshman in 1944, Ursuline's enrollment sat at a record high of 710, and Father Gallagher was one of the institution's most beloved figures. "I'll never forget Fr. Gallagher," Sister Isabel recalled. "He would stand at the top of the stairs…saying 'hello' to everyone in the morning."[59]

The gregarious priest was no less admired by members of the Ursuline religious community, with whom he established a strong working relationship.

In 1936, graduates of Ursuline High School posed before the campus's convent. They were led in a procession by top students of the junior class, including future bishop James Malone, the student seen wearing a white suit. *Courtesy of Father Richard Murphy.*

Shortly after his appointment as the high school's principal, Father Gallagher took up residence at the Wick Avenue convent and regularly said morning mass for the sisters at the Rayen Street convent, located about a mile south of the high school. On January 10, 1946, while engaged in one of those morning errands, the priest's car was struck by another vehicle that apparently went through a nearby red light. Father Gallagher was killed instantly.[60]

Reports of Father Gallagher's death sent shockwaves through Ursuline High School, and "students wept openly upon hearing the news."[61] To fill the sudden void in leadership, Sister Rosemary Deibel was appointed as the school's interim principal, a position she held until Father Glenn W. Holdbrook took over the following month. A solemn wake held at the Wick Avenue convent drew thousands of mourners, and a steady stream of memorials focused on the priest's dedication to the high school, as well as his role in its recent development.

Without detracting in any way from Father Gallagher's contributions, one might acknowledge that the growth of Ursuline High School conformed to a larger pattern of development, one that had turned a vibrant Catholic community into the seat of a new diocese.

Finding a Place in a New Diocese

On June 4, 1943, an area of Northeast Ohio—including Stark, Columbiana, Mahoning, Portage, Trumbull and Ashtabula Counties—was canonically established as the Diocese of Youngstown. The new diocese, which comprised 3,404 square miles, hosted several major manufacturing and steel-production centers and large stretches of agricultural territory. In *The March of the Eucharist from Dungannon*, a commemorative volume published eight years later, the Diocese of Youngstown claimed 110 churches, three hospitals and two schools of nursing operated by religious orders.

The volume's author, the Most Reverend James A. McFadden, first bishop of Youngstown, wrote with clear conviction that "[t]he Diocese of Youngstown is well established and is developing a vigorous Catholic life in opposition to the evil forces which would destroy our country."[62] The bishop's triumphalist tone probably went unnoticed in the early 1950s, when the Mahoning Valley's economic and cultural vitality appeared boundless.

Since the beginning of the twentieth century, the story of the Youngstown area had been a narrative of continuous growth. The city's population more than tripled between 1900 and 1920, soaring from 44,885 to 132,358.[63] In 1925, a *Vindicator* survey showed that the population had risen to 161,477,[64] while engineers at Ohio Bell predicted Youngstown's population would reach 470,000 by 1950 if growth continued at the same pace.[65]

In an era of exponential development, urban institutions of all kinds thrived, including Youngstown's parish schools, which numbered fifteen by the end of the 1920s. Within a decade, despite the challenges brought on by the Great Depression, the community boasted a total of nineteen parochial elementary schools staffed by seven religious orders and enrolling about 6,750 children.[66]

Following America's entry into World War II and the revitalization of the local steel industry, the city's population, which peaked in 1930, hovered at around 170,000.[67] Given these circumstances, the carving of a new diocese from what had been the larger Diocese of Cleveland surprised few observers. Indeed, by the spring of 1943, Youngstown resembled nothing less than the seat of a Catholic diocese, due in part to the efforts of the late Father Edward Mears, who predicted that the church he built would "one day be a cathedral."

In the late 1920s, under the pastorate of Monsignor Joseph N. Trainor, the impressive third edifice of Saint Columba Parish was enhanced by the installation of two copper spires that were modeled on those of the

With the establishment of the Diocese of Youngstown in June 1943, the former parish of Saint Columba became a cathedral. *Courtesy of Diocese of Youngstown.*

Cathedral of Norwich in England.[68] Once the spires were in place, the stately church rose 140 feet above Wood Street, forming "a conspicuous part of the downtown skyline."[69] Long regarded as "one of the finest churches in the old Cleveland Diocese," Saint Columba Cathedral was expected to serve as an "impressive setting" for the installment of a new bishop.

Bishop McFadden, a native of Cleveland, described his appointment as spiritual leader of the new diocese in terms that were refreshingly personal. As a youth, he often visited relatives in the Mahoning Valley, and the *Vindicator* indicated that he regarded his new assignment as a homecoming.[70]

As the bishop settled into his "second home," the Ursuline Sisters played a role in his transition. Closely associated with the newly designated cathedral parish, the religious community enjoyed a comfortable relationship with the episcopal leader, a familiar face at Saint Columba over the years.

Mother Blanche Klempay, then serving as the superior, generously invited the new bishop to live with the Ursulines at their Wick Avenue convent, where Father Gallagher, the principal of Ursuline High School, was already in residence. "Bishop McFadden said early Mass for the sisters every morning and Msgr. Andrew Prokop, his secretary, came every morning and evening to have meals with him," noted Ursuline chroniclers Sister Anne and Sister Mary Ellen. "When the sisters needed help, it was common for the Bishop to say, 'Andy will do that for you.'"[71]

While Bishop McFadden's cordial relationship with the Ursuline Sisters owed much to their years of service at Youngstown's premier parish, there is little doubt he appreciated their long record of achievement.

CUTTING A PATH IN CATHOLIC EDUCATION

The new bishop probably knew that between the early 1880s and late 1920s, the Ursulines had opened at least eleven parish schools, including Saint Columba, Saint Ann, Immaculate Conception, Saints Cyril and Methodius, Saint Rose, Saints Peter and Paul, Holy Name of Jesus, Sacred Heart of Jesus, Saint John the Baptist, Saint Charles Borromeo and Saint Nicholas.

In September 1905, the same year the community opened Ursuline Academy, Sister Helen Wernet became the founding principal of Saints Cyril and Methodius School, an institution that served a mainly Slovak American community on Youngstown's north side. Nine years later, in September 1914, Sister Alphonsus McCabe served as the first principal of Saint Rose School, which was connected to a territorial parish in neighboring Girard.

The following year, in September 1915, Sister Florence Gilboy opened Saints Peter and Paul School, which served a mostly Croatian American community on the city's north side. Just five years later, in 1920, Sister Elizabeth Kupec became founding principal of Holy Name of Jesus School, based in a Slovak American enclave on Youngstown's west side.

Three years later, in 1923, Sister Celestine Duffy opened Sacred Heart of Jesus School, located in a working-class neighborhood on the city's east side. Then in 1926, Sister Dolores Waldman became founding principal of Saint John the Baptist School in nearby Campbell.

The following year, in 1927, Sister Helen Wernet opened Saint Charles Borromeo School in Boardman. (Twenty years after the school's closure in 1932, it reopened under the leadership of the Ursuline nuns.) Three years later, in 1930, the Ursulines opened Saint Nicholas School in neighboring Struthers.

In 1927, students at Youngstown's Saint Francis of Assisi School were taught by (*left to right*) Sister Kathleen Kelly, Sister Christine Carroll and Sister Laurentina Butler. *Courtesy of Ursuline Sisters of Youngstown.*

Finally, in September 1944, less than a year after the establishment of the Diocese of Youngstown, Sister Louise McGraw reopened Youngstown's Saint Patrick School on the south side, which had been staffed by the Cleveland-based Sisters of Saint Joseph.[72]

An obscure chapter in the community's history involves the establishment in 1927 of Saint Pancratius Hall, a short-lived boarding school for boys located on U.S. Route 224 in Canfield. The school closed in 1929, and the site served for the next fifteen years as Glen Garda, a recreational center for the Ursuline Sisters.[73]

Significantly, the Ursulines continued to provide teaching services to local parish schools during the worst years of the Depression, even though conditions prevented them from receiving much in the way of compensation. A striking example of this pattern involved Immaculate Conception School, which served dozens of working-class families on the city's east side.

Immaculate Conception's well-known financial difficulties can be traced back to a 1929 fire that devastated the school building and left the parish

$89,000 in arrears.[74] The parish's predicament, while extreme, reflected the kinds of challenges many churches faced as they struggled to maintain schools amid shrinking contributions.

Evidence that the problem was widespread among local parish schools can be found in news reports suggesting that some parishes were unable to cover even the modest salaries of religious instructors. In a 1935 *Vindicator* article, Monsignor William A. Kane, then the dean of the Mahoning Valley clergy, observed: "State aid will be absolutely necessary to continue the work of the parochial schools.…The situation is very bad at the present time, although the parishes are doing their best to keep them going."

The article stressed that parochial schools were "unique in that [their] only source of revenue is through the contributions of parishioners." The newspaper's description of conditions at one hard-hit local parish may refer to the situation at Immaculate Conception. "In one parish, where approximately 50 percent of the parishioners are now out of work, the contributions are 70 percent less than they were four years ago," the article stated. "It has been impossible for the parish to pay the sisters, although the salary of each is but $50 a month."[75]

Although Youngstown's steel-centered economy picked up after the United States entered World War II, Immaculate Conception remained a struggling parish community. In 1941, the parish recorded about eight hundred families, most of whom were dependent on the modest wages of blue-collar workers.[76]

Sister Virginia McDermott, who taught at the school, explained that about six hundred students were enrolled at Immaculate Conception in the early 1940s. The breadwinners of these families were "working in the mills, and rather poor." She observed that the school's mostly Irish and Italian American families were so accustomed to poverty that few bothered to conceal their plight. "I always loved Immaculate Conception, and I loved… the openness of the people to you," Sister Virginia recalled. "They were poor. And they were a wonderful example of how to live simply because they all did."[77]

Although Immaculate Conception emerged intact from the Depression and World War II, it was anything but a thriving enterprise. The parish's postwar challenges included massive debt and a decaying physical plant, and its financial difficulties were alleviated only slightly by the frugal policies of Father Joseph McCann, who assumed the pastorate in 1941.[78]

Decades later, Sister Virginia described a conversation between Father McCann and Sister Mary Alice Ryan, in which the priest indicated he was determined to compensate the sisters for their services. "He said [that] he owed a debt to the Ursulines that…was a huge debt from years back," Sister Virginia recalled. "And Fr. McCann said, 'I will not go to my grave without paying that debt to those sisters.'" In the end, the aging pastor was unable to keep that promise.

After Father McCann's death in 1954, he was replaced by a younger priest, Father Arthur DeCrane, who was forced to address the parish's long-neglected maintenance issues. Father DeCrane asked the community to forgive the parish's longstanding debt and launched a fundraising drive to restore the parish's aging infrastructure. Hence, the debt to the religious community ultimately went unpaid.[79]

This was not the only case in which the Ursuline Sisters of Youngstown had effectively subsidized a troubled parish school by providing teaching services without compensation.

Nevertheless, by 1944, the Ursuline community's stellar reputation as educators had attracted scores of young women who were inspired by the prospect of teaching in religious schools. With the convent on Rayen Avenue again overcrowded, the community, under the leadership of Mother Paul Townley, set out to acquire another building. In time, Mother Paul became aware of a property in nearby Liberty Township, a structure that would become the grandest of the community's motherhouses.

FROM NIGHTCLUB TO MOTHERHOUSE

In the mid-1940s, the former Henry K. Wick home rose from a wooded stretch of Liberty Township's Logan Avenue like a misplaced European manor house. Its Gothic-style interior featured "high ceilings, grand staircases, and arched leaded glass windows." Yet the fifty-four-room mansion had long ago ceased to function as a private residence.[80] Over time, it had become a relic of the Mahoning Valley's industrial "golden age," an era in which steel, iron and coal magnates mimicked the lifestyle of European aristocrats.

The home's abandonment was scarcely the outcome its builders envisioned. In 1911, when local industrialist Henry Wick and his wife, Millicent, were planning the mansion, they drew up the blueprints "in such a way that [upon their respective deaths]…the edifice could quickly be [remodeled] to serve as a city art gallery which was then needed badly."

The Wicks spared no expense on their luxurious home, which was built at a cost of $480,000 and occupied a six-hundred-acre estate that had been purchased for another $600,000. The *Vindicator* reported that the home's furnishings, which included a valuable art collection, were "worth a quarter of a million [dollars]."[81]

In the end, the couple's carefully laid plans were undermined by circumstances beyond their control. Henry Wick, already in his early seventies when the project began, died five years after its completion. While his young widow continued to collect precious works of art, her economic situation deteriorated with the onset of the Depression. In 1934, not long after announcing that the mansion and its contents would be auctioned off, Millicent Wick invited local reporters "for an afternoon tea and final tour of her huge home."[82]

Shortly thereafter, Wick relocated to California to live with her son from a previous marriage, bringing along a handful of treasured items. Overnight, it seemed, the Wick Mansion had been transformed from an architectural treasure to a "white elephant."

Then in the summer of 1935, a trio of investors appeared to come to the rescue with a plan to reinvent the mansion as a "public eating place and recreational center." Business partners G.R. Homan, Thayer T. Wood and Joseph Newton took out an extended lease on the property and made modifications that would render the home a suitable entertainment destination.[83]

Known as the Mansion, the nightclub was managed by entrepreneur Tony Cavalier, the owner of the fabled Elms Ballroom on Youngstown's north side. Longtime political leader Harry Meshel, who worked at the Mansion as a teenager, recalled that the club hosted major acts, including the Ink Spots, the Andrews Sisters, the Duke Ellington Band, the King Sisters and "the remnants of the Glenn Miller band."[84]

After a memorable run in which the Mansion became "the most popular spot for young couples within a 50-mile radius," the nightclub lost its momentum.

This time, the area's Junior League stepped in, convinced that the former estate would be an "idyllic scene" for an outdoor summer concert series led by Michael Ficocelli, a prominent local conductor. The concert series, which ran for three summers, featured outdoor dancing on a large terrazzo dance floor that had been installed by the proprietors of the Mansion.[85]

By that time, real estate developers, who had been eyeing the property for some time, purchased about 570 acres of the original estate for a development known as Norwick Village. Given these circumstances, the future of the elegant old mansion seemed more precarious than ever.

In May 1945, Youngstown bishop James McFadden blessed the new motherhouse of the Ursuline Sisters on Logan Avenue. *Courtesy of Ursuline Sisters of Youngstown.*

Then in May 1944, the *Vindicator* announced that the Ursuline Sisters had arranged to purchase the former residence—an investment that required them to sell Glen Garda, their recreational center, to the Pious Society of Saint Paul, an Italian-based order of priests that established a presence in the United States in the 1930s.

Representatives of the real estate company indicated the development of Norwick Village, which had been "halted by Pearl Harbor," would be carried out "in co-operation [*sic*] with the Ursulines." N.T. Hurd, a representative of the Wick estate in the negotiations, stressed that "landscaping, laying out roadways and establishing zoning restrictions will be done with reference to the desires of the religious community."[86]

In its coverage of the sale, the *Vindicator* observed that the building "was very limited in its possible uses," a situation that enabled the religious community to purchase the lavish structure (along with thirty-one acres of land) for just $33,000. The former residence was then "reconditioned to accommodate 60 nuns and to serve as a novitiate."[87]

Bishop McFadden confers with Sister Coletta Braun and Mother Paul Townley at the 1945 blessing of the community's motherhouse. *Courtesy of Ursuline Sisters of Youngstown.*

On the afternoon of Sunday, May 27, 1945, the new motherhouse was blessed by Bishop McFadden in a dedication ceremony attended by "officers of the Ursuline community, novices, postulants, and as many professed sisters as can be accommodated." The ceremony opened with a blessing of the building's exterior, after which the bishop led a large procession to the main section of the convent, where he offered a "special benediction."

Later, the bishop, accompanied by Father H. Leo Collins and Father Joseph McCann, blessed each of the structure's fifty-four rooms, "ending with the chapel." The ceremony concluded with a ritual blessing of an American flag donated by U.S. congressman Michael J. Kirwan, an influential political leader.

The next morning, on Monday, May 28, 1945, Bishop McFadden sang a pontifical high mass at the motherhouse, accompanied by Monsignor Joseph Trainor, who served as archpriest; Father Maurice Casey, who acted as deacon; and Father John G. Hamrak, who acted as subdeacon.

Liturgical music at the ceremony was provided by the Ursuline Nuns Choir, with Sister Veronica Labuda directing and Sister Evelyn Croell accompanying the group on the organ. Afterward, the Ursuline Sisters of Youngstown issued a formal statement that emphasized their longstanding commitment to the area: "The Ursuline community, established here in 1874, is a peculiarly Youngstown institution. It has grown with the city…and has always taken an active part in its civic, educational, and religious life."[88]

After the pontifical mass, the new motherhouse was officially closed to the public, and a new chapter in the history of a storied area landmark would begin.

3

POSTWAR TRANSFORMATION

Few events triggered a more dizzying array of changes within the Mahoning Valley than the end of World War II, and many of these developments would have unintended consequences. Still, it should come as no surprise that the area's residents greeted news of the war's conclusion with unbridled optimism.

On the evening of August 15, 1945, more than 30,000 Youngstown-area residents swarmed into the city's Central Square to mark V-J Day, while hundreds of others gathered at local churches, temples and synagogues. To prepare for the anticipated onslaught of celebrants, municipal officials dispatched 165 police officers, who were "augmented by 96 auxiliary police, 100 firemen and some 9 military police from Cleveland, all of whom… within a matter of a half hour faced a seething, milling mass of laughing, screaming, sobbing humanity in Central Square."

The *Vindicator* observed that on the previous evening, hundreds of worshippers had gathered at nearby Saint Columba Cathedral "to express thanks to the Almighty at the close of a period frightful in the history of mankind." In a homily, Youngstown bishop James McFadden described the war's conclusion as "a victory for the great causes for which our men and women fought."[89]

The Ursuline Sisters shared the public's openness to the possibility of a better future—and they soon had reason to be hopeful. The post–World War II baby boom, which fueled a rise in the community's population, boosted enrollment at local parish schools, which, in turn, filled classrooms at Ursuline High School.

This 1952 photograph of downtown Youngstown, taken at West Federal and Hazel Streets, captures the atmosphere of the postwar era. *Courtesy of Mahoning Valley Historical Society.*

During the late 1940s, the secondary school's rolls swelled to nearly 1,200, and its reputation grew accordingly. From Ursuline High School's beginnings as a small private school for girls, it had evolved into a large coeducational institution whose alumni held leadership positions throughout the area.

In 1950, the bright, forward-looking students who staffed the high school's yearbook committee seized on the popularity of an emerging technology to present their class's experience in the format of a television show. "The senior class of 1950 asks that you tune your television sets to the Ursuline channel," the yearbook's introduction began. "On the screen of the Ursulinian they will attempt to project the story of their life at Ursuline."

Not content to simply exploit the novelty of television, the editors of the *Ursulinian* aimed for a tone of gravity. "You will note one great difference between this presentation and an ordinary TV show," the introduction stated. "This is performance with a purpose. The purpose? Not entertainment, but construction. A rehearsal for life—that's what one might call this show."

The introduction described Pope Pius XII as the television production's "supreme director" and presented Bishop McFadden as "chief control engineer." It went on to introduce Bishop Coadjutor Emmet M. Walsh as "special effects engineer" and Father Glenn Holdbrook, the school's principal, as "the man in the control room."[90]

In contrast, the Ursuline Sisters, who had founded the school and comprised nearly 90 percent of its teaching staff, received little attention. Under the heading "Educational Amplifiers," the nuns were acknowledged on a single page that included an alphabetized list of their names and one-word descriptions of their disciplines. While numerous images of clerical leaders, including pastors of local parishes, filled the yearbook, the publication contained no photographs of Ursuline Sisters.

This presentation diverges sharply from the impressions of alumni like Father John Mulqueen, who attended the school between 1949 and 1953. "At the time, the faculty was almost entirely composed of nuns," he recalled. "The handful of lay teachers at the school included Tom Carey, who then served as the school's coach." Father Mulqueen suggested that the Ursuline Sisters played a key role in an experience that he presented as "the best four years of my life."[91]

Perhaps the invisibility of the teaching nuns reflected their own sensibilities, given that they were members of a formal religious community and treated their contributions as a service to the diocese. No less significant was the fact that the Ursulines had surrendered many of their former administrative duties when the school was turned into a coed institution.

At the same time, by 1950, diocesan leaders were showing a stronger interest in Ursuline High School, and their plans crystallized in 1952, after the death of Bishop James McFadden and the installment of his successor, Bishop Emmet Walsh. In 1953, one year after his appointment, Bishop Walsh presented a proposal to Mother Blanche Klempay to purchase the school from the Ursuline community.

As part of the arrangement, the diocese promised to assume the order's $102,000 debt, while overseeing the construction of a new addition "to meet the anticipated influx of students." The terms of the proposal indicated the high school "would retain the name of the Order in its title, and the Ursulines would remain the sole community of religious women to staff the school."

The new bishop's actions revealed a broader interest in the project of Catholic secondary education. Even as he pursued his plan to purchase Ursuline High School, Bishop Walsh called for the creation of a second high school to be named in honor of the late Edward Cardinal Mooney, a former Youngstown resident who had served as the archbishop of Detroit.

Unlike Ursuline, Cardinal Mooney High School would be staffed by several religious orders, including the Villa Maria, Pennsylvania–based Sisters of the Humility of Mary, the Cleveland-based Sisters of Notre Dame, the Pittsburgh-based Vincentian Sisters of Charity, the Akron-based Dominican Sisters and, of course, the Ursuline Sisters of Youngstown.

To strengthen the appeal of his proposal, Bishop Walsh also promised to support a drive to build a new motherhouse for the Ursuline Sisters, whose community was evidently outgrowing the former Wick Mansion in Liberty Township.[92]

In 1954, the Ursuline Sisters agreed to the sale of the high school, and a contract was ratified by the apostolic delegate to the United States, Archbishop A.G. Cicognani, in December that year. "A great era of private

A statue of Saint Angela Merici, the founder of the religious community, once graced the interior of the convent at Ursuline High School. *Courtesy of Ursuline Sisters of Youngstown.*

administration and ownership passed with the sale," one historical account noted. "The era of the central diocesan high school in the Diocese of Youngstown had begun." Yet no one questioned "the central contribution of the Ursuline Nuns to Ursuline High School."

Work on the school's new addition (designed by local architect P. Arthur D'Orazio) began in the fall of 1954 and was completed about a year later.[93] In the end, the arrangement did not work as smoothly as the Ursuline community anticipated. The diocese proved slow to pay off the community's sizable debt, and an initial payment was not made until 1960, at which point a considerable amount of interest had accrued. That same year, the sisters were taken aback when Bishop Walsh proposed a "joint fundraising effort" that would not only finance the new motherhouse but also cover construction costs at Ursuline and Cardinal Mooney High Schools.[94]

The Growing Need for a New Motherhouse

Meanwhile, the Ursuline Sisters, who staffed many of the diocese's religious schools, continued to deal with a situation in which their members were dispersed among three major residences: the nineteenth-century convent on West Rayen Avenue, the former Andrews Mansion at Ursuline High School and the motherhouse on Logan Avenue.

Sister Isabel Rudge, who entered the novitiate before completing her senior year at Ursuline High School, shared her impressions of conditions at the former Wick mansion in Liberty Township. Struck by the building's grandeur, she was nevertheless aware that the motherhouse posed certain challenges. Its cavernous rooms were lined with gleaming wood paneling, which the novices were expected to polish regularly.

Furthermore, given the huge dimensions of many of the structure's bedrooms, the Ursuline Sisters needed to take imaginative steps to accommodate younger members of the community. "The bigger rooms on the floor up…had been turned into four or five rooms, with [the hanging of] curtains," she explained. "You didn't have walls."

Additionally, the motherhouse's winding staircases, with their plush carpeting, presented a challenge to some of the older nuns in residence. Sister Isabel estimated that forty sisters and novices were living in the motherhouse during the period of her novitiate. "There were two separate dining rooms, for the sisters who were already professed and the novices," she noted.

At sixteen years of age, Sister Isabel was the youngest member of her novitiate, but her peers weren't much older, and at times, their behavior reflected their tender age. The young novices periodically attended a class led by a priest from Canfield's Saint Paul Monastery, who spoke with a thick Italian accent. "He delivered a talk on religious vows, but because he was speaking from his Italian side, he called them 'wows,'" she recalled. "So, if you get ten people who are in that age bracket—sixteen and up—we used to laugh." She acknowledged that this behavior stood in sharp contrast to the formal atmosphere of the novitiate.[95]

The formality of the motherhouse was softened to some extent by the community's support of its members' artistic aspirations. Occupants of the building were often treated to classical music, thanks to the efforts of Mother Paul Townley, who organized the religious community's orchestra in the 1940s. "Sisters got instruments from wherever they could—friends, family, pupils," one commemorative history noted. "Several times a week, during study or recreation, the Sisters went off into parts of the house to practice their instruments." On special occasions, the Ursuline Orchestra performed for an audience, "which was always receptive, of course."

Overall, it is difficult to ignore the sheer number of Ursuline Sisters who showed outstanding artistic talent. Years before Mother Paul established the Ursuline Orchestra, the community won recognition for its ambitious theatrical productions. In 1935, Sister Joan Gerlach sponsored a well-received "dramatic art production" to mark the four hundredth anniversary of the order's establishment by Saint Angela Merici in 1535.

Meanwhile, Ursuline High School's theater program benefited from the contributions of other talented directors, including Mother Charles Hoffman, Mother Vincent O'Connell and Sister Rosemary Deibel. The visual appeal of Sister Rosemary's theatrical productions was enhanced by the design work of Sister Alice Marie Morley, a graduate of the Pius X Institute in Florence, Italy, who led the school's art department.

Equally significant was the role that individual nuns played to bring classical music to a larger audience. Notable figures included Sister Blessed Sacrament Whelan, Sister Genevieve Kelly, Sister Xavier Rudge, Sister Frances DeSales McDade and Sister Cecilia Morano.[96] In some ways, the elegant motherhouse on Logan Avenue was an ideal setting for a community known for its celebration of beauty and artistry.

Initially, the grounds of the motherhouse were secluded, as the mansion sat a considerable distance from the main road. "When I was first there, there was one lane that [stretched] from Logan [Avenue]…up to that big

An Ursuline Sister reflects on an image of the Sacred Heart of Jesus at the motherhouse. *Courtesy of Ursuline Sisters of Youngstown.*

Two Ursuline Sisters and a novice relax on the leafy grounds of the motherhouse. *Courtesy of Ursuline Sisters of Youngstown.*

estate," Sister Isabel observed. "It was quite a drive from Logan [Avenue] up to that house."

While the district had retained a measure of its pastoral charm, change was in the air, and large stretches of the township were already being developed. Sister Isabel indicated that two streets had been established just north of the motherhouse, and each was soon lined with attractive new homes.[97]

Over time, the encroachment of new housing made the former estate a less attractive venue for the Ursuline Sisters. "Two boundaries began to close in on the nuns during the fifties," the *Vindicator* noted in a retrospective article. "Their order began to outgrow the mansion and houses along Redfern and Wildfern Drives and Virginia Trail were built closer and closer."[98] The development of Liberty Township, which impinged on the community's privacy, reflected a much larger pattern of suburbanization that was draining urban areas of their residents.

THE IMPACT OF SUBURBANIZATION

In 1954, the *Vindicator* estimated that Youngstown's population had risen modestly to 168,330, a gain of merely 610 residents. The newspaper indicated these meager gains reflected "one of the biggest population shifts in Youngstown's history," a massive movement of people to the suburbs.

Based on its survey, the newspaper reported, "nearly all the major cities in a five-county area around Youngstown have failed to record much population growth in the last fourteen years but…outstanding increases have been noted in areas bordering on the municipalities." Significantly, the survey also revealed that the adjoining suburbs of Austintown and Boardman saw their respective populations double during the same period.[99]

This trend was driven, in part, by government programs that largely benefited white families, as Black families were systematically excluded from most suburban communities. Many white families, however, benefited from the generous terms for home loans offered by the Federal Housing Administration (FHA) and Veterans' Administration (VA). "These agencies revolutionized home ownership in the United States," historian Steven M. Gillon noted.

In the past, "prospective homeowners had to produce a significant down payment, often 50 percent or more, and pay off the rest of the loan in less than ten years," he added. During the postwar era, however, government agencies like the FHA and VA "required only a 10 percent down payment and allowed homeowners to pay off the mortgage over thirty years at a low interest rate."[100]

While the Youngstown area's population trends would have a profound impact on the community's parochial schools, local Catholic leaders were slow to grasp the long-term implications of suburbanization. The postwar baby boom's positive effect on enrollment in the city's parish schools evidently encouraged false hopes among urban Catholic educators, as declining neighborhoods were temporarily infused with new life.

Media accounts suggest diocesan representatives were generally optimistic about the future of Catholic education. In the mid-1950s, the *Vindicator* reported that "based upon the number of infant baptisms, the Youngstown Catholic Diocese must be ready to meet more than a 50 percent increase in elementary school enrollment, alone, by 1960."[101]

In response to rising enrollment levels, parishes throughout the community refurbished and expanded parochial school facilities. In 1952, for example, the Ursuline Sisters opened the new edifice of Saint Columba School, built at a cost of $195,000. The fireproof building, which replaced its nineteenth-century predecessor, stood directly behind the cathedral.

Monsignor James A. "Jay" Clarke, a retired priest who once served as diocesan chancellor and vicar of clergy, shared his impressions of the new school, which he first encountered as a third-grade student. "What was amazing about that new school was that it was so modern compared to the old one," he recalled. "They had an intercom system, and the voice of Sr. Mary Agnes [Convery], the principal, came over the first intercom system that we had ever heard…and actually, we were a little bit afraid of her."[102]

Several years later, Immaculate Conception Church's new pastor, Father Arthur DeCrane, launched a fundraising campaign to secure money for the repair of the school and church facilities, a project he hoped to complete before the parish's seventy-fifth anniversary in September 1957.

By the time of the celebration, Father DeCrane had "succeeded in painting and decorating the church, modernizing the rectory, remodeling the school to add classrooms and kitchen facilities in the original building as well as constructing an addition."[103] Despite such material improvements, however, the pastor probably recognized that his parish was steadily losing its most valuable resource: its parishioners.

This pattern may have escaped the attention of less-engaged observers, given that the neighborhood's declining Catholic population was not initially reflected in the parish school's enrollment levels. In 1955, Immaculate

Sister Margaret Mary McCabe bakes altar bread at the convent on West Rayen Avenue.
Courtesy of Ursuline Sisters of Youngstown.

Conception School was holding its own with 535 students enrolled, retaining its place as the city's third-largest parish school in terms of enrollment. Yet this figure, while only slightly lower than enrollment numbers recorded in the 1940s, seems unsettling when one considers that the postwar baby boom was fueling explosive growth elsewhere in the city. During the mid-1950s,

Local conductor Michael Ficocelli (*left*) presides over a flutophone lesson for fourth-grade students at Saint Rose Elementary School in Girard, while Sister Jerome Corcoran (*right*) looks on. *Courtesy of Ursuline Sisters of Youngstown.*

enrollment at Youngstown's Saint Patrick School, a southside institution that had been staffed by the Ursulines since 1944, rose by one-third, as student numbers soared from 800 to 1,204.[104]

However, the relatively high numbers recorded at Saint Patrick also proved deceptive. Due to factors that included suburbanization, the school's junior high annex, built in 1955 to accommodate a growing student population, was forced to shut down twelve years later.[105] As historian Glen Gabert Jr. noted, the percentage of Catholics who were sending their children to parochial schools declined sharply, even as enrollment figures were pushed upward by the population increase of the baby boom.[106]

In time, the disquieting changes unfolding within the city were compounded by the effects of urban renewal and highway construction, which destabilized dozens of neighborhoods. For some Catholic residents looking back on this period, a harbinger of the city's transformation was the shocking destruction of one of its most cherished landmarks.

"OUT OF THE ASHES"

For five decades, the granite, neo-Gothic edifice of Saint Columba's Church dominated a bluff overlooking Youngstown's downtown retail district. The parish, which operated the city's oldest parochial school, was described as a "fortress of the faith," a phrase that reflected the local Catholic community's defensiveness at the time the building was completed in 1903.[107]

This wariness was reinforced by the distrust and intolerance shown by "old stock" Anglo-Americans during the late nineteenth and early twentieth centuries. As late as the 1920s, the rise of a local chapter of the Ku Klux Klan came in response to an earlier influx of southern and eastern European immigrants, many of whom were Catholic.[108]

Yet, by the time Saint Columba's was designated as a cathedral in 1943, interreligious tensions had largely subsided, and most area residents, regardless of background, viewed the landmark as a local architectural treasure.

On September 2, 1954, a fire broke out in the cathedral's choir loft around 9:30 p.m., not long after the building was struck by lightning during a violent storm. There were no witnesses to the outbreak of the fire, which blazed undetected for an hour and a half before a passerby happened to notice the flames.[109]

Monsignor James Kolp, an associate pastor at the cathedral parish, was reportedly the first person to contact the fire department. "It was on a Thursday evening, and I had finished hearing confessions at the cathedral," the priest recalled. "I returned to the rectory, where a gentleman had asked to speak with me in the office. Suddenly, the doorbell rang, and when I responded, someone screamed, 'The church is on fire!'"

After calling the fire department, the priest briskly alerted another associate, Father William Picard. "We went over to the church, obtained the key to the tabernacle, and quickly removed the Blessed Sacrament," he explained. "At that time, the fire was not yet very strong in the altar area of the cathedral."[110]

By the time firefighters arrived on the scene, flames had engulfed the cathedral's organ and choir loft, eerily illuminating the building's massive rose window. Those on hand were alarmed by evidence that the fire was creeping along a catwalk and loft that ran the entire length of the cathedral's nave.

Firefighters realized that if the massive timbers of the ceiling and roof were to catch fire, the blaze would burn out of control, reducing the cathedral to a shell. Their efforts to contain the blaze in the choir loft ultimately failed,

The destruction left by a 1954 fire at Saint Columba Cathedral is suggested in this image of the ruined cathedral's Altar of Mary. *Courtesy of Mahoning Valley Historical Society.*

and the firefighters watched helplessly as the blaze "spread across the roof toward the rear of the building."[111]

When the blaze was finally contained, at around 2:30 a.m., Saint Columba Cathedral was ruined and presumed to be a total loss. Within hours, Bishop Walsh calculated the damage to the cathedral at "more than $1,250,000," adding that insurance would cover just $940,000 of rebuilding expenses.[112]

In the fire's immediate aftermath, religious services were held at a nearby armory, which was outfitted to serve as a makeshift chapel. Sister Isabel Rudge recalled that a funeral service for her uncle Leslie Rudge, who had passed away shortly after the cathedral's destruction, took place in the unassuming building.

Weeks later, she added, services were moved to Youngstown's southside, where the neo-Gothic edifice of Saint Patrick Church served as the pro-cathedral while Saint Columba was being rebuilt.[113]

The fire came as a personal tragedy to Sister Isabel and other Ursuline Sisters who felt a strong connection to the cathedral parish.

Then on April 12, 1959, less than five years after the destruction of the old cathedral, a new structure was dedicated on the site. For many Catholics around the diocese, however, the new cathedral came as a second shock, as it could not have been more different in design and dimension than the one it replaced. A 1997 anniversary booklet for the cathedral parish described the building:

> *The new cathedral was noteworthy for its simplicity of design. Statues were "replaced with bas-reliefs over the altar. Pastels and neutral tones in mosaic and marble make for a bright and airy structure. More modest dimensions called for a central aisle of 102 feet as opposed to the 130-foot-long Gothic church. The sanctuary was significantly smaller, 44 X 49 feet, as opposed to the 78-foot-wide sanctuary in the old cathedral. The exterior of the new cathedral was a cream Mankato stone."*[114]

The new building's most striking quality was its self-consciously modern style, which stood in stark contrast to the neo-Gothic style of its predecessor. Not surprisingly, local Catholics, who viewed the former cathedral as a cherished icon, showed mixed reactions to the new building, whose appearance struck many of them as unfamiliar, even alienating.

On a Sunday morning in the fall of 1958, when Father Glenn Holdbrook sang the first high mass in the new cathedral, he appeared to speak to these reservations as he compared the new edifice to the reconstructed temple of King Solomon in the Old Testament. "On the day of the viewing…the young men and women stood in amazement and open awe at the beauty of the new building," Father Holdbrook told the assembled congregants. "But the old men and women sat down and cried because the temple did not compare to the old place of worship."[115]

Notably, the designer's decision to eschew the medievalist aesthetic that characterized much of U.S. Catholic architecture before World War II reflected a sea change that had occurred within the American church itself, a shift that would become more apparent in the wake of the Second Vatican Council a few years later. Thus, in certain ways, the destruction and rebuilding of Saint Columba Cathedral presaged the theological and liturgical changes of the post-conciliar era that helped transform American Catholicism.

These changes, in combination with the social and political upheavals of the 1960s, would undermine the post-Tridentine brand of Catholicism that had thrived in America since the mid-nineteenth century.[116] The local Catholic community was entering a period of swift and expansive change, and the Ursuline Sisters would reflect and, in some cases, lead those changes.

The second edifice of Saint Columba Cathedral, dedicated in 1959, was markedly different in design and dimension than its predecessor. *Courtesy of Thomas Welsh.*

"A NEW BREED"

Looking back, Sister Nancy Dawson asserted that her years at Immaculate Conception School in the late 1940s played a crucial role in her religious formation, even though she was exposed to a largely devotional form of Catholicism. "We went to Mass all the time, and especially during the Lenten… season and all the holy days," she explained. "One [thing] I always remember was All Souls Day, because if you said your six 'Our Fathers,' your six 'Hail Mary's,' [and] six 'Glory Be's,' you would get a soul out of Purgatory."

These practices were reinforced within the Dawson household. "There was always great devotion to the Blessed Mother," Sister Nancy observed. "We always had a Marian altar…and, of course, we always had the crowning [of the Blessed Virgin] in the school.…To this day, I've maintained some of those practices."

While most of Sister Nancy's instructors at the parish school were Ursuline Sisters, she developed particularly close relationships with three members of the religious teaching staff: Sister Mary Alice Ryan, Sister Virginia McDermott and Sister Gabriel Manley. "They had compassionate hearts," she recalled. "If I didn't feel well, [Sister Mary Alice] told me to put my head down on the desk. I didn't have to worry about anything."

By the time she graduated from Ursuline High School in 1955, Sister Nancy was leaning toward a service-oriented profession. She thought about entering the field of nursing and even considered joining a missionary religious order. Yet unlike most of her peers who were pondering a vocation, Sister Nancy refrained from entering the convent after graduating from high school. "I didn't answer until I was twenty-one, because my dad asked me to wait," she explained. Instead, Sister Nancy took an office job at a local steel company and enrolled at Youngstown State University, where she eventually earned a bachelor of science degree in education.

As she considered her next step, Sister Nancy consulted with Monsignor Breen Malone, who served as diocesan vocations director, and Sister Regina Schneider, both of whom offered the kind of "broader view" she appreciated. Sister Regina had piqued Sister Nancy's interest in a missionary religious order, and she found herself moving in that direction when Monsignor Malone unexpectedly asked, "Have you thought about the Ursulines?" "I'd never thought about being a teacher," Sister Nancy admitted. "I just remember saying to him, 'There has to be more than this.'"

Even as she contemplated a commitment to religious life, however, Sister Nancy maintained a lifestyle that was typical of a young person of her generation. She spent most of her spare time socializing and even looked for a job in New York City, a cultural hub she visited at least once a year.

Then one Thanksgiving Day in the late 1950s, she met with Mother Blanche, the community's superior, who accompanied her to the Ursuline Motherhouse and initiated her entrance into the novitiate.

On a brisk January evening in 1959, Sister Nancy drove up the motherhouse's winding driveway, flinging her "last" cigarette out the car window. Fresh from a dance class, she was wearing a leotard and sported a ponytail that ran down the length of her back.

When she entered the neo-Gothic building, she spotted a familiar face among the nuns who greeted her. Without thinking, she blurted out that she remembered seeing the woman at a popular entertainment spot. A sudden chill descended on the room. "Everyone was just holding their breath," Sister Nancy recalled. "There was a very strict environment."

Like many of her peers, Sister Nancy was overwhelmed by the elegance of the motherhouse. "[I remember] those beautiful stairs," she said, adding that members of her class posed for photographs on the winding staircase after taking their final vows. "It was…kind of a romantic setting…that speaks of being a spouse of Christ," she noted.

Sister Nancy soon found, however, that the motherhouse—for all its beauty—functioned somewhat as a gilded cage. "When we first went in there, we didn't go home at all," she observed. "We didn't use the phone at all.…You had visiting with relatives once a month.…There was still that isolation from family."

This separation placed a special burden on Sister Nancy's father, Francis, who, unlike her staunchly Catholic mother, Hannah, had been raised outside any specific faith tradition. In the end, Sister Nancy found the restrictions on her interaction with family members the most troubling aspect of her novitiate.

Significantly, her novitiate dovetailed with a period of imminent change within the Catholic Church, and the events that ensued would have far-reaching implications for those involved in religious life. "In those years, the thing that started to change was an understanding of the *charism* of the community," Sister Nancy observed. "There was a spirituality that was more contemplative in the beginning. There was a…scheduled prayer routine that was more monastic."

In time, as she researched the origins of the Ursuline community, she encountered a story that surprised her. "Angela [Merici] really worked with laywomen…and laymen in her life," she stressed. "So, the initial roots were

Above: Ursuline Sisters interact with family members during "Visiting Sunday," a monthly opportunity to meet with relatives. *Courtesy of Ursuline Sisters of Youngstown.*

Left: Sister Martina Casey, a postulant, poses with her uncle T. Leo Casey and his wife, Jane, on the grounds of the motherhouse. *Courtesy of Ursuline Sisters of Youngstown.*

not contemplative at all. However, there was a period in which the Ursulines were cloistered, and their role was determined by the bishops."

In the fertile era leading up to the reforms of the Second Vatican Council, Sister Nancy was drawn to the work of Thomas Merton, an American Trappist monk whose 1948 autobiography, *The Seven Storey Mountain*, had created a stir within religious circles. "He inspired me a lot in my own vocation, because he was so human and so sinful and…traveled the world," she noted. "In the novitiate, we had a library, but I thought that was one of the books you weren't supposed to read—and I remember sneaking it out of the library."[117]

At the time, Sister Nancy could scarcely have imagined that she would one day witness—even facilitate—dramatic changes within her own religious community.

4

ON THE BRINK OF CHANGE

The early 1960s were a period of unprecedented hope for thousands of American Catholics. On the international stage, Pope John XXIII, defying predictions he would serve as a mere caretaker, "stunned the world by calling an ecumenical council" intended to "throw open the windows of the church to the modern world."[118] In a departure from the past, the council initiated by Pope John welcomed the contributions of thinkers who had been thrown into "ecclesiastical exile" by Pius XII. Their efforts imbued Catholicism "with a new sense of the church moving through history…and directly addressing the problems of the current age."[119]

If the new pope "continued to challenge the atheistic materialism and totalitarian ways of world communism," he also "abandoned ritual denunciations and initiated dialogue with communists," while directing criticism "with greater force at western cultural imperialism and liberal capitalism." Historian James Hennesey, Society of Jesus (SJ), observed that for Americans who "expressed their Catholicism largely in terms of emotional anti-communism or uncritically accepted the assumptions of the American and Western economic system, an era had ended even before the Second Vatican Council began."[120]

On the domestic political scene, the 1960 election of President John F. Kennedy "suggested more than any proclamation could that Catholics at long last were comfortably integrated into American society."[121] The results of the U.S. presidential election were greeted with enthusiasm in Youngstown, a working-class community with a substantial Catholic population. Less than

Future president John F. Kennedy greets area residents during a campaign stop in October 1960. *Courtesy of Mahoning Valley Historical Society.*

a month earlier, on October 9, 1960, Kennedy had paid a visit to the city, addressing a huge crowd in downtown's Central Square.[122]

The young candidate's awareness of Youngstown probably reflected its political and economic importance, as the city was then a crucial northeastern Democratic stronghold.[123] Many of those who gathered in Youngstown's central square that afternoon, however, appeared to feel a personal connection to the candidate: a coreligionist who took pride in his immigrant roots.

This was true of Sister Patricia McNicholas, a high school student at the time of the presidential race pitting Kennedy against Richard M. Nixon. She indicated that most of her peers at Cardinal Mooney High School shared her enthusiasm about the prospect of a Catholic president. Like many of her classmates, she wore a button emblazoned with the slogan, "If I were twenty-one, I would vote for Kennedy."

Sister Patricia recalled that Kennedy's inauguration, on Friday, January 20, 1961, coincided with a skiing expedition organized by Cardinal Mooney's

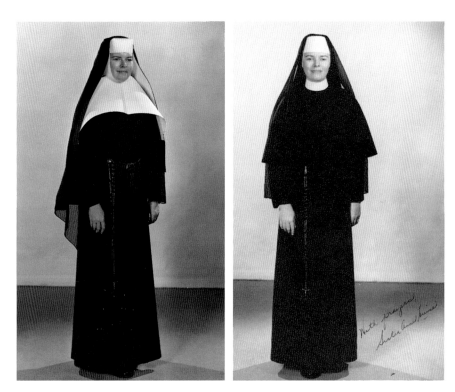

In 1962, Sister Marcia Welsh presented the community's modified habit. *Courtesy of Mahoning Valley Historical Society/Vindicator Printing Co.*

assistant principal, Father David Lettau. Students had the day off, and Sister Patricia described "coming down from the slopes" and entering the ski lodge just in time to watch Robert Frost read his poem "The Gift Outright" in a live broadcast of the inauguration.

She added, however, that the memory was bittersweet. At the time, Sister Patricia was mourning the loss of her father, Paul James McNicholas, who had passed away the previous year from the long-term effects of a disabling injury. In the wake of her father's death, Sister Patricia began to think about a religious vocation. "The reality of suffering that I knew as a child made me interested in seeking some kind of meaning," she explained.

While she had established a positive relationship with the Dominican nuns who taught at Cardinal Mooney, Sister Patricia felt drawn to the Ursuline Sisters. "When I chose the Ursulines, it was…out of a sense of this city," she explained. "The Ursulines were based here in town." Her respect for the order was encouraged by her mother, Mary Frances

McNicholas, who maintained close friendships with Sister Perpetua White and Sister Virginia McDermott.

By the time Sister Patricia entered the convent in 1962, sweeping reforms were in the air, but few of them had been implemented. "So, I was totally received into that old religious life," she recalled. "I'm the last group that got that formal habit. At those early days of sister formation, we were still learning about an old-style religious life."

She acknowledged that a handful of changes was being carried out in six-month stages, and some members of the community were reading Leon Joseph Cardinal Suenens's *The Nun in the World*, a book then considered groundbreaking. This piecemeal approach to reform, however, contributed to an atmosphere informed by uncertainty. "There was a…disjointed sense of what we were all about," Sister Patricia noted.[124]

BUILDING A NEW MOTHERHOUSE

During the second year of Sister Patricia's novitiate, the religious community began the laborious process of vacating the motherhouse on Logan Avenue. The move came as no surprise, given that the possibility of building a new facility had been raised in the mid-1950s, when the religious community sold Ursuline High School to the Diocese of Youngstown. At the time, diocesan officials even proposed 1960 as a possible date for a fundraising campaign to benefit the construction project. As it turned out, plans for the project moved forward shortly after Mother Edna Marie Brindle's election as superior on the projected date of 1960.

By then, the housing situation for the Ursuline Sisters had become a challenge. "The convents in which the sisters were currently living were very inadequate," one historical account observed. "The Rayen Avenue convent, which had been built in 1897, was now significantly overcrowded, with serious fire hazards; the Logan Avenue convent housed the novices and the administration; and the Wick Avenue convent was overflowing."[125]

The first step in planning a new motherhouse was to secure a parcel of land on which to build it. To this end, Mother Edna Marie and members of her council spent most of their weekends visiting potential sites in Youngstown and its surrounding suburbs. They finally settled on a 130-acre piece of land in Canfield, which was bordered by Shields and Messerly Roads to the south and east, respectively, and Raccoon Road to the west.

Despite their previous understanding with the diocese, the community's leaders determined that "buying the property should be independent of the promised diocesan fundraiser." They consulted with an advisory committee composed of local business and civic leaders, including Dr. John McCann, attorney John Newman, Dr. John Scarnecchia, John Hutch, Fred Shutrump Sr., James Griffin, Charles Cushwa, John Coakley, P. Arthur D'Orazio, William G. Lyden and Anthony P. O'Horo. This committee launched a fundraising campaign that eventually raised $115,000 to purchase and prepare the site.

From there, the Ursulines selected P. Arthur D'Orazio as the architect of the new motherhouse and Fred Shutrump, the president of Charles Shutrump and Sons Co., as the contractor. The subcontractors for the project included Beil Electric Co. and Crogan Plumbing and Heating Co.

To fund the building's construction, the Ursulines participated in the scheduled diocesan fundraising drive between March 20 and June 30, 1961. Planned by Bishop Emmet Walsh "to aid both the Catholic high schools and the Ursuline Motherhouse," the fundraiser's success was enhanced by the participation of the Ursulines, who "solicited money from their relatives and friends, personally visiting homes of potential contributors." In the end, the Ursuline Sisters received 50 percent of the funds raised in Mahoning County, a figure totaling $282,000.

Construction of the new motherhouse began in 1962 under the supervision of Mother Edna Marie, who was assisted by Walter "Wally" Pascarella, a master painter and the brother of Sister Victoria Pascarella.[126] The project proceeded quickly, and the building was finished in December 1963.

By then, the religious community had sold off the Rayen and Logan Avenues convents for $46,753 and $105,500, respectively. Money raised from the sales "was used to buy furnishings for the new Motherhouse, supplementing the usable furnishings from the other convents."

As it turned out, however, the community's expenses exceeded their resources. When calculating the total funds available for the motherhouse's construction—including the $200,000 owed by the diocese (along with accrued interest), the $282,000 raised through the campaign and the community's own savings—the Ursuline Sisters found there was still a deficit of $578,000.

That balance was covered through a loan from the Chicago-based financial firm of McMahon and Hoban Co., with an understanding that it "would be paid off through the sisters' efforts by 1974, the 100th anniversary of the Ursulines' coming to the Mahoning Valley."[127]

In line with this goal, the community announced plans to operate a preschool in the vicinity of the motherhouse, a project the *Vindicator* described as "their first source of private income since Ursuline High School and the Wick Ave. property were transferred to the Youngstown Diocese."[128]

As the Ursuline Sisters prepared to relocate to the new motherhouse, they benefited from the donated services of four moving companies, including J.V. McNicholas Transfer Co. The move from Logan Avenue took place on December 13, while the Rayen Avenue convent was vacated on December 18, 1963.[129] "Much of that fall, we were packing up the building," recalled Sister Patricia, whose novitiate began at the old motherhouse on Logan Avenue.

She recalled that the move to Shields Road overlapped with a national tragedy, given that President Kennedy had been assassinated in late November. At the time, the television set was covered with boxes filled with items bound for the new building. "We never watched it, except when President Kennedy was killed in November," Sister Patricia explained. "They actually cleared the boxes, and we got to watch a little bit of it, whereas the rest of the world was glued to their television sets."

The new Ursuline Motherhouse in Canfield reflected a mid-century modern aesthetic. *Courtesy of Ursuline Sisters of Youngstown.*

The somber tone of the news coverage deepened the women's feelings of apprehension as they pondered the move. "We liked it [at Logan Avenue], because it was just the novitiate," Sister Patricia observed. "Coming here, suddenly, there were all these other people." She compared the tiny sleeping quarters at the new motherhouse to those of a college dormitory.

Such reservations meant little to Mother Edna Marie, who greeted the novices when their bus reached the new motherhouse. Aware that the local media would be on hand, the general superior urged the novices to feign enthusiasm. As Sister Patricia recalled, "[She] got on the bus and said, 'The cameras are all out here in the front—smile!'"[130]

While not everyone was satisfied with conditions at the new $1 million motherhouse, the religious community's leaders evidently believed that the order would benefit from the concentration of most of its members in one facility for the first time since the late nineteenth century.

Built on a 117-acre plot, the airy, two-story motherhouse could accommodate 115 sisters and novices. The building's ground floor featured a lobby and parlors, a chapel, administration offices, a study room, a community room, dining rooms, a kitchen and laundry, sleeping quarters, a college wing and a special wing for the novitiate. The motherhouse's second floor hosted an infirmary, dormitories for novices and additional sleeping quarters for professed sisters.

Like the rebuilt cathedral, the new motherhouse's chapel conformed to a mid-century modern aesthetic, as architect P. Arthur D'Orazio had eschewed a more traditional approach to design. The sole exception to this pattern was the chapel's altar, which incorporated an item salvaged from the ruins of the first edifice of Saint Columba Cathedral: a marble bas-relief of the Last Supper.

Meanwhile, the Second Vatican Council's overarching theme of engagement was reflected in the religious community's decision to hold an ecumenical open house for Protestant ministers, Jewish rabbis and their wives on May 9, 1964. Subsequent open house events were held for members of the Century Club, a group of major donors to the Ursulines (May 14, 1964); sisters from other religious orders who were active in the Mahoning Valley (May 16, 1964); and members of the public (May 17, 1964).[131]

The community's leaders soon discovered that local interest in the facility was greater than they had anticipated. On Monday, May 18, 1964, the *Vindicator* reported that sixteen thousand vehicles were involved in a traffic jam the previous day, as thousands of area residents showed up for the public open house. "Motorists who parked on both sides of the road caused

Ursuline Sisters gather in the lobby of the new motherhouse during the May 1964 dedication ceremony. *Courtesy of Ursuline Sisters of Youngstown.*

the traffic jam," the newspaper stated. "Some got stalled in the soft berms, [others] had overheated engines, and a few ran out of gasoline."

Vehicles involved in the traffic jam "were backed up to Lockwood Blvd.," located more than two miles away, and "hundreds of persons walked to the grounds." Those gathered at the motherhouse, who ranged "from three to 90 years of age," were "kept…in good humor" by the "all-star parochial band which played on the lawn." The article attributed the huge turn-out, in part, to "balmy weather," noting that the last guest departed at 10:15 p.m., "long past convent hours."[132]

Space and parking considerations were likely a factor in the community's decision to limit attendance at the motherhouse's dedication to "superiors of other religious orders and members of the Ursuline lay advisory board."[133] Despite the relatively small crowd, the ceremony, held on Sunday, May 24, 1964, received detailed coverage in the local media.

The dedication ceremony opened with a pontifical mass led by Youngstown bishop Emmet Walsh, who was assisted by Monsignor Walter Martin, the pastor of Sacred Heart Parish (Youngstown), as deacon; and

Monsignor John Lettau, a diocesan chancellor, as subdeacon. When the mass ended, Bishop Walsh led a procession around the community's chapel that included "approximately 70 priests from area churches, the nuns and laymen." The bishop then proceeded to bless crucifixes that hung in every room of the motherhouse.[134]

After the dedication, the Ursuline Sisters turned their attention to the retirement of the community's sizable debt. They received critical assistance from members of their original advisory committee, who, along with forty like-minded colleagues, had organized the Century Club. The club's founders "devoted many hours securing members who would pledge $100 a year until the remaining $578,000 construction debt was paid," and their efforts were complemented by those of another group, called the Soli Deo Gloria Club.

Meanwhile, between 1964 and 1968, the Ursuline Sisters held an annual fundraising event known as the Lawn-A-Rama, a festival that took place on the grounds of the motherhouse. "Sisters sold admission tickets and chances," one historical account noted. "Parishes sponsored booths selling ice cream and cake, hot dogs and baked goods." Profits generated by the event typically ranged from $9,000 to $10,000.

The Lawn-A-Rama was supplemented by an indoor fundraiser known as the Fall Festival, which was held at Ursuline High School between 1962 and 1969. Once again, local parishes were invited to set up booths featuring games, novelties and refreshments. The festival generated anywhere from $15,000 to $20,000.

Notably, the debt for the motherhouse's construction was retired in 1972, the final year of Mother Edna Marie's term as general superior.[135] Improvements to the motherhouse were completed over the next several years.

In 1965, local contractor O'Horo financed the construction of an outdoor pool at the back of the facility, insisting it would benefit the sisters' overall health. When it fell into disuse during the winter months, O'Horo "offered to enclose the pool as a Christmas gift."

At the same time, it had become increasingly apparent that the motherhouse's swampy grounds required the introduction of some kind of drainage system. Under the supervision of the community's maintenance man, Leo Rotkowski, an effort was launched to dig a 1.9-acre lake on the property.

Completed with the assistance of army engineers and representatives of the Ohio Department of Agriculture, the man-made lake "outflowed into a pipe that went across Route 62 and emptied into a drainage area called Anderson Run." The lake was stocked with small-mouth bass and bluegills, thanks to the efforts of Sister Jeanne Cigolle and Sister Veronica Labuda, "who traveled miles to pick them up 'for free' from a government source."

Subsequent improvements included the construction of a curving driveway exiting onto Messerly Road, a project completed in the late 1960s.[136] By the end of the decade, the new motherhouse on Shields Road not only served as a modern home for the Ursuline Sisters but also stood as a shining testament to the support the community enjoyed in the Youngstown area.

Leaders in Education

By the early 1960s, Ursuline High School had won local recognition for its outstanding theater program, which had been developed under the leadership of Sister Rosemary Deibel. In December 1963, the veteran instructor took charge of the high school's annual Christmas show, organized under the theme "Joy to the World."

Ursuline's Thespian Society and Glee Club collaborated on the show, which included a one-act play, a "nativity tableau" and a performance of Christmas songs. One key participant in the show was a senior student named Ed O'Neill, known then for his achievements on the gridiron, as well as his rare ability to tell a funny story.

Fifty years later, the Hollywood actor revealed that Sister Rosemary had "recruited" him for the show's one-act play, which was titled *The Three Wise Guys*. "When she asked you to do something, you were drafted," O'Neill recalled. "She said, 'I want you to do this, and you'll be good at this.' I don't recall her saying, 'You'll be helping us out, and I appreciate it.' This was not a request."

O'Neill stressed, however, that Sister Rosemary was generally pleasant and supportive. "I remember that I liked her," he said. "At the same time…she kept charge of her classroom, and not with any kind of physical discipline. There was something about her demeanor."

Written by a member of the school's faculty, *The Three Wise Guys* is a one-act play about a group of hoodlums who wander into a church on Christmas Eve and encounter a young boy kneeling before a crèche. The hoodlums, or "wise guys," notice that the boy is wearing expensive clothing and begin to ridicule him.

The situation threatens to become violent when the boy suddenly reveals that he is blind. At that point, two of the hoodlums exit nervously, leaving

Future Hollywood actors Ed O'Neill (*left*) and Jim Cummings (*center*) participate in a 1963 holiday play directed by Sister Rosemary Deibel. Also shown is student actor Rosemary (Zeck) Prine. *Courtesy of Ursuline High School.*

"No, Mickey, wise men, not wise guys."

the ringleader, a character named "Mickey," alone with the boy. After an awkward pause, the boy asks Mickey to kneel and pray with him in front of the crèche, and it soon becomes clear that the gang leader is weeping.

Looking back, O'Neill recognized that Sister Rosemary showed great skill in her casting of the play. The role of Mickey went to a senior named Bobby Mansfield, who enjoyed a reputation for his physical toughness. Other members of the trio included student athletes Joseph Sammartino and David Wienberger, while the boy's mother was played by Rosemary Zeck, a leader within the student body.

Supporting roles were given to Ted Alexander and John Ricci, while the critical role of the young boy was assumed by future Hollywood voice actor Jim Cummings, then a precocious eleven-year-old who lived next door to Ursuline High School.

Although Sister Rosemary had invited O'Neill to participate in the speech program's oratorical division during his junior year, his appearance as a senior in *The Three Wise Guys* was his first genuine theatrical experience. "It was interesting that Mother Rosemary pegged me for the [role of the] priest," the actor observed. "This woman saw something in me that I didn't see in myself.…Well, I did see it, but it was vague."

His unacknowledged interest in acting was reflected mainly in his obsession with films. "Under Mother Rosemary's influence, [this interest] took on a different form and a different import," O'Neill explained. The impact of his initiation into acting was heightened by the fact that *The Three Wise Guys* received an unusual amount of publicity. The play was not only performed at Ursuline High School but also taped by WKBN, a television station that aired it for local viewers.

O'Neill would not act again until 1969, when his hopes of a career in professional sports were unexpectedly dashed. "When I got back to Youngstown after being cut by the Pittsburgh Steelers, I became aware of the Youngstown Playhouse," he noted. O'Neill then studied acting at Youngstown State University, where he appeared in numerous productions of YSU's Spotlight Theater before relocating to New York City.

Years after his departure, O'Neill made a point to drop in on his former instructor during a visit to Youngstown. "She was very sweet and encouraging, as usual," the actor recalled. "Mother Rosemary was my first influence, and she took me seriously.…That's what got the ball rolling for me.…It had to be."[137]

Meanwhile, Hollywood actor Jim Cummings, best known as the voice of Winnie the Pooh and Tigger in the Walt Disney Company's animated films, starred in two productions of *The Three Wise Guys*. Initially recruited to play the role of the boy in the autumn of 1963, he was later cast as the gang leader in the school's December 1969 production of the play.

Like O'Neill, Cummings was impressed by Sister Rosemary's dedication to her craft. "She was a great lady, but she would toe the line with you, in the name of good education and proper guidance," he said. "She and her good friend, Sister Alice Marie [Morley], the art teacher, were peas in a pod." He pointed out, however, that Sister Rosemary was never forceful. "She would always cajole you through the process," he said.

The high point of his theatrical career at Ursuline was his involvement in the school's production of Rodgers and Hammerstein's *The King and I*, widely regarded as Sister Rosemary's most successful turn as a director. Cummings gave Sister Rosemary credit for pushing him to further develop his talents. "She saw the potential in her students and cultivated it, and she allowed that talent to blossom," he stated.[138]

Such testimonials to the long-term influence of Ursuline educators are commonplace, even though the subsequent careers of O'Neill and Cummings may seem extraordinary. Indeed, by the 1960s, the religious community's members were regarded as leaders within the local educational sector.

The Ursuline Sisters' commitment to excellence in teaching was evident early on. Starting in the late 1920s, the community's members benefited from specialized training at Cleveland's Sisters' College (later known as Saint John College) and Ursuline Normal School, an institution staffed by local sisters and priests. A select number of Ursuline Sisters also completed coursework at The Catholic University of America, including Sister Regina Schneider, Sister Charles Hoffman, Sister Veronica Habuda, Sister Mary Louise McGraw, Sister Rosemary Deibel and Mother Blanche Klempay.

In time, more novices attended classes at Youngstown College, later known as Youngstown State University. In June 1959, the media covered the graduation of forty members of the religious community from the local institution. Four years later, with the establishment of an educational wing at the new motherhouse, the Ursulines "obtained an affiliation with… Youngstown State University to hold college classes in this wing."

The program's faculty included instructors with formidable credentials, including Sister Anne Lynch and Sister Mary Catherine Doran, who held graduate degrees in mathematics and social studies, respectively, from Peabody College for Teachers in Nashville, Tennessee. While members of the Ursuline community were the primary beneficiaries of the education program, students also included a group of Oblate Sisters from Trumbull County, who had arrived from Italy in the 1950s.[139]

During this period, the Ursuline Sisters were well represented among the area's elementary and secondary schools. Members of the community staffed thirteen parish schools in Youngstown and surrounding Mahoning County, including Saint Columba, Immaculate Conception, Sacred Heart, Saints Cyril and Methodius, Saints Peter and Paul, Holy Name, Saint Patrick, Saint John the Baptist (Campbell), Saint Charles (Boardman), Saint Nicholas (Struthers), Holy Family (Poland), Saint Luke (Boardman) and Saint Joseph (Austintown).

Elsewhere in the diocese, they provided teaching services at Saint Rose (Girard), Saint Patrick (Leetonia), Saint Joan of Arc (Canton), Immaculate Conception (Wellsville) and Our Lady of Lourdes (East Palestine).

Additionally, Ursuline Sisters taught at both of Youngstown's diocesan high schools. Significantly, Ursuline High School's most celebrated educators included four graduates of The Catholic University of America: Sister Winifred Melody, English; Sister Regina Schneider, science; Sister Marie Celine Olejar, counseling; and Sister Rosemary Deibel, French, Latin, English and speech.[140]

Furthermore, the school's art department was led by Sister Alice Marie Morley, who had received a scholarship to study art in Florence, Italy, during the 1958–59 school year.[141] Similarly, Sister Helen Shea, an English instructor who served as an assistant principal, held a degree from the University of Notre Dame.

Ursulines who enriched the curriculum at Cardinal Mooney High School included Sister Margaret Ann Klempay, who established an art program; Sister Elizabeth Kerrigan and Sister Jude Yablonsky, who developed a journalism program and produced musical theater shows each spring; Sister Anne Lynch, who introduced a modern math program; and Sister Barbara Turk, who taught biology.[142]

Notably, Sister Mary Conroy enriched the English programs at both diocesan schools, with her credentials including a graduate degree in English from Marquette University and a doctorate in Black literature from the University of Notre Dame.

Not surprisingly, the influence of the Ursuline Sisters was also felt at the diocesan level, and the career of Sister Jerome Corcoran illustrates their broader impact on Catholic education. After earning a doctorate degree in education from Case Western Reserve University in 1954, Sister Jerome served for several years as a diocesan supervisor and assistant superintendent of schools.

As a writer and researcher, Sister Jerome made significant contributions to the scholarship about Catholic education through the publication of two books: *The Elementary School Principal* (1961) and *The Pastor and the School* (1966), coauthored with John P. Tracey and Justin A. Driscoll. Both publications caught the attention of Catholic educators, and Sister Jerome "traveled extensively giving lectures on their content."

Sister Jerome's years at the diocesan office coincided with the tenure of Sister Bernardine Fickers, a diocesan administrator in student guidance, then referred to as "pupil personnel." During this time, Sister Marie Hughes, in her capacity as a supervisor of religious education, organized a diocesan office to develop catechetical classes for public school students.

In 1957, Sister Marie implemented the program known as Confraternity of Christian Doctrine, or CCD, which was designed to offer Catholic students at public schools a religious education comparable to that received by their parochial school counterparts. In 1966, Sister Marie was succeeded by Sister Mary Ann Coz, who became the religious education office's primary supervisor. Other diocesan educational supervisors included Sister Marie Helene Chismar and Sister Rita DeChello.[143]

Even as they remained active in area classrooms, the Ursuline Sisters participated in diocesan efforts to recruit lay instructors in response to a looming teacher shortage. In 1961, the diocese launched a cadet teacher education program that was designed "to attract lay teachers to the parochial school system and to enable them to get good professional methods and college degrees." The challenge of recruiting lay teachers was complicated by the fact that parochial schools were unable to provide wages competitive with those offered by public schools.

At the time, most prospective lay teachers were women, and the Brothers of Christian Instruction were then limited to teaching male students. Hence, the Ursulines assumed control of training classes held at Youngstown State University and Canton-based Walsh College, respectively.

Aspiring teachers who enrolled in the program benefited from the combined experience of such instructors as Sister Mary Ellen Dean, Ohio history and western civilization; Sister Rosemary Deibel, speech; Sister Alice Marie Morley, art; Sister Helen Shea, English; Sister Germaine Staron, music education; Sister Mary Catherine Doran, history and social studies methods; Sister Anne Lynch, mathematics; and Sister Mary William Yurko, content subjects.[144]

If these accomplishments were not enough, the religious community had earned recognition for its local contributions to early childhood education. By the mid-1960s, it was clear that the Ursuline Sisters' entrance into the area of preschool instruction was a success. Given the public's positive response to the preschool, few recalled that the project faced initial opposition.

Mother Edna Marie Brindle's original plan to open a community-sponsored preschool on the motherhouse grounds met with Bishop Walsh's firm disapproval. In a show of determination, the general superior reimagined the project as a private enterprise, formed a committee and identified a possible site that was located across the street from the motherhouse on the corner of Shields and Racoon Roads.

The property, then owned by former stage actress Lillian Desmond Ranz, included a mansion and five and a half acres of land. With the assistance of attorney John Newman, the community opened negotiations with Ranz and arrived at what they considered a mutually satisfactory figure. At that point, however, the retired actress surprised everyone. "This is my property and I'm free to do what I want with it," Ranz insisted. "I choose to give it to the Ursuline Sisters for a school for young children."[145]

Ursuline Preschool opened to the public on September 8, 1963, with 115 students enrolled in the nursery school and kindergarten.[146] Sister Edith

In 1964, students at Ursuline Preschool were greeted by principal Sister Edith Weir (*far right*), along with Sister Marianna Sacamoni and Sister Paula Kisan. *Courtesy of Ursuline Sisters of Youngstown.*

Weir, the school's principal, led a faculty that included Sister Paula Kisan and Sister Mary Sacamoni. Within a couple of years, Sister Gabriel Manley and Sister Mary Edward Durkin also joined the teaching staff. By the end of the decade, a steady rise in student enrollment led to the building of an addition that served as an auditorium/playroom.[147]

Despite these encouraging trends, however, Catholic education was on the cusp of changes that would eventually transform the Ursuline religious community itself.

Mass Exodus

Sister Norma Raupple was, in many ways, typical of the young women who were drawn to religious life in the early 1960s. A product of the postwar baby boom, she had been raised in a leafy neighborhood on Ridgewood Drive, a suburban thoroughfare that ran through a developing residential section of Boardman Township.

Sister Raupple's father, Dr. M. Carl Raupple, was a prominent physician, while her mother, Clarita (Harbison) Raupple, was a homemaker. As the oldest of five children, she often babysat her younger siblings and assisted her mother with household chores.

Sister Norma described her parents as religious, conscientious and community-oriented. "My dad, as a general practitioner, was on call twenty-four hours a day and seven days a week for deliveries, the emergency room and house calls," she noted. "With my dad's help, my mom held everything together at home."

Like many children of her generation, Sister Norma grew up in a neighborhood brimming with younger families. Yet Sister Norma especially enjoyed the time she spent with her teachers at Saint Charles Elementary School. "I stayed after school and helped the sisters," she said. "I loved Saint Charles."

While still in elementary school, Sister Norma began to consider a religious vocation. "My dad's generosity and availability to the public had a huge impact, in terms of modeling service," she said, adding that her mother's dedication to her family left an equally strong impression.

Sister Norma's attraction to religious life was enhanced by her experiences at Father Kane's Camp, a recreational facility in Lake Milton Township that was operated by the Diocese of Youngstown. The camp was staffed by Ursuline nuns, and Sister Norma, a junior counselor, enjoyed numerous opportunities to interact with them.

Then, as a student at Cardinal Mooney High School, she was further exposed to religious women through a Jesuit-run youth program called Catholic Action. "We went on a bus to Pittsburgh one summer, and we visited Chicago another summer," she explained. "The sisters were with us, so a lot of that [experience] was relational, building bonds and seeing them as happy people."

She was especially drawn to what she saw as the Ursulines' focus on the needs of the community. "The main ingredient was service…to others," she said.

Sister Norma entered the Ursuline community in the spring of 1964, shortly after the opening of the motherhouse in Canfield. Her family's home in Boardman sat less than four miles from the new facility, and she rode her bike from Ridgewood Drive to Shields Road. "We were the first group that…entered into the new motherhouse," she explained.

Like Sister Patricia McNicholas, a member of the preceding class, Sister Norma encountered a religious community in a state of transition. Although the Ursulines had implemented a few minor changes, including a recent modification of their habit, they upheld a range of traditional policies, including strict limits on the amount of time novices could spend with their relatives. "I was homesick," Sister Norma recalled. "The Sunday visiting with family wasn't all that great because, with my dad's schedule and four kids at home, they were often late."

A more pressing concern for Sister Norma, however, was the steady departure of her classmates from her novitiate. "I made final vows in 1972, which was just fifty years ago," she recalled. "I think seventeen of us joined, while three of us made final vows, and the other two left shortly afterward. Nobody in our present community was with the group I joined, and that was right in line with the big exodus as Vatican II was unfolding."[148]

Sister Norma's experience coincides with that of Sister Regina Rogers, who entered three years later in 1967. Born in the largely Italian American village of Lowellville, Ohio, Sister Regina was raised in Poland Township, a suburban community that featured little ethnic or racial diversity.

While Philip and Caroline (Delisio) Rogers attended mass regularly, Sister Regina indicated that her mother was particularly religious. "She cherished the treasures of the faith," she noted. "We said the Rosary in October and May without my father."

Sister Mary Alyce Koval (*center*) gathers with family members, including her aunt Sister Mary Volk, as she prepares to take her final vows. *Courtesy of Ursuline Sisters of Youngstown.*

From an early age, Sister Regina was drawn to religious environments. During the summer months, when the Ursuline Sisters returned to their motherhouse in Canfield, she followed their instructions and assisted the priests at her parish. "Every day, I would go down [to church] and…put out the vestments for mass for the next day," she noted.

Sister Regina's formative years were spent at two parochial schools, both of which were staffed by Ursuline Sisters. After studying for three years at Saint Nicholas School in nearby Struthers, she enrolled at the relatively new primary school maintained by Holy Family Parish, which had been established in Poland during the late 1950s.

At Holy Family, Sister Regina came to idolize her fourth-grade teacher, Sister Mary Ellen Dean, then known as Sister Suzanne. She described Sister Mary Ellen, who passed away in 2022, as "one of the kindest people I ever knew." "There was just something about her presence that was calming, peaceful," she added. "Those are the qualities she transmitted to others around her, and she didn't know how much of an influence she exerted on other people."

When Sister Regina entered the Ursuline novitiate, however, she was shocked at the traditional atmosphere she encountered. Despite the influence of Vatican II elsewhere in the Catholic community, the environment at the motherhouse remained surprisingly strict. "We didn't mingle much with the professed [members of the community]," she explained. "It wasn't until near the end of my novitiate that I got to spend time with them." Much of this quality time took place when she drove older members of the community to medical appointments. "That's when I got to talk to them about when [they] were young," she recalled.

Like Sister Norma, she established positive relationships with members of her novitiate class, but she was distressed to find they were reconsidering religious life. "My unhappy memory would be that…there were seven of us who entered," Sister Regina observed. "By the time of first profession, I was the only one remaining.…Lots of women were leaving religious communities across the country, and this was true of the Ursulines, too."[149]

Writers and researchers seeking to explain this phenomenon have pointed to various factors, including the growing secularization of American society and an overlapping increase in employment opportunities for women unaffiliated with religious communities.

Many observers have also suggested this trend can be seen as an unintended consequence of the Second Vatican Council. Harold A. Buetow, in his pioneering history of Catholic education, pointed out that the council's central document, "*Guadium et Spes*" ("The Church in the Modern World"), "evidenced a positive concern for the whole world"—a sharp departure from the insular perspective of the past.[150]

Similarly, former *New York Times* religion editor Kenneth Briggs argued that Vatican II's new emphasis on civic engagement coincided with a shift away from a traditional hierarchical model of the church that minimized the role of the laity. This model was displaced by a more inclusive vision of the church as "the people of God," which diminished the special status once accorded to clergy and the religious.

Thus, Vatican II "flattened the playing field regarding vocations, lowering the status of a nun or upgrading the vocation of marriage, depending on your perspective."[151]

In Briggs's view, this change in status, combined with other controversies of the post–Vatican II era, fueled a decline in vocations starting in the late 1960s. Briggs stressed that, at the same time, a growing number of sisters set out "to fulfill the highest aims of 'Gaudium et Spes' for justice and service to the world." In the process, they turned "their energies away from certain kinds of activities such as teaching in Catholic schools in favor of projects to combat racism, feed the hungry, and find shelter for the homeless."[152] This trend would have profound implications for Catholic education.

Yet these were not the only developments affecting religious life in the decade of the 1960s. In June 1967, Sister Marie Augusta Neal, SND, the director of the research committee for the Conference of Major Superiors of Women (now the Leadership Conference of Women Religious), initiated a survey that included almost four hundred congregations around the country. In a project intended to analyze the beliefs and attitudes of religious women in the wake of Vatican II, each congregation was directed to distribute survey questions "covering every aspect of religious life."

Mother Edna Marie enrolled the Ursuline Sisters in the study, and Sister Jerome oversaw their participation. Once the survey had been submitted, "several community meetings were held explaining the results of the [study] and encouraging the sisters to implement the findings."

The project paved the way for the Ursulines' pursuit of "the self-study advocated as a follow-up to Vatican II." Ursuline communities were encouraged "to hold special chapters in which they were 'to go back to their roots'…and to evaluate their present constitutions in the light of the Vatican II directives."[153]

Sister Julia Baluch recalled that she found a careful review of her community's history illuminating. "[Our founder] was Angela Merici…a woman far ahead of her time," she explained in an interview. "She didn't want the women in a…convent. She didn't want them in identifiable garb. They were to live at home, dress modestly, in the [fashion] of the day…. Then, after her death, things began to change." She added, "Here, we were doing the same thing. We were discussing our rules, our constitution."[154]

Hence, a religious community long known for its commitment to elementary and high school education was poised to reinvent itself.

MIXED MESSAGES

Sister Isabel Rudge's educational career conformed to the path that was taken by many Ursuline Sisters of her generation. In the late 1940s, even before she was a professed member of the Ursuline community, she found herself teaching classes at Saint Nicholas School in Struthers, where she served from 1949 to 1952.

From there, she moved on to Youngstown's Saint Patrick School, where she taught from 1952 to 1955. That same year, Sister Isabel returned to Saint Nicholas, where she taught until 1957. Finally, she was transferred to Ursuline High School, where she served between 1957 and 1977, spending her final years there as an administrative assistant.

During her first decade at Ursuline, Sister Isabel lived at the former Andrews Mansion, a remnant of the Gilded Age that stood in the middle of campus. "There was a beautiful dining room, but we never used it," she recalled. "We served the priests breakfast there when they came to [say] mass."

The mansion's centerpiece was an elegant wooden staircase that led to the second floor. "For the [senior] prom, you had to get your picture taken [there]," Sister Isabel said, noting that local brides also competed to be photographed on the staircase. Other highlights of the convent included hand-crafted woodwork and stained-glass windows. "The flooring had been beautiful, but by this time, if you put too much water on the first-story floor, it was down in the basement," she explained.

The old convent on Ursuline High School's campus was razed in 1968, and a new facility was opened the following year. The new building, a modest two-story brick structure, drew complaints from some teaching nuns, who indicated their rooms were too small.

Over time, more sisters expressed concerns about temperature control at the new facility, recalled John Ulicney, an Ursuline alumnus who had returned

The former Chauncey Andrews Mansion served as a residence for religious instructors at Ursuline High School until it was pulled down in 1968. *Courtesy of Ursuline Sisters of Youngstown.*

to teach at his alma mater. "At the new convent, you had two brick walls with no insulation in between them," Ulicney noted. "The convent was cold in the winter and hot in the summer—not a good situation for the sisters."

The instructor also lamented the razing of a historical landmark in a community that was rapidly losing its architectural heritage. "You had this beautiful building that was treated as an eyesore," he observed ruefully.[155]

Overall, however, the youthful teacher viewed Ursuline High School as a dynamic, well-managed institution. Ulicney, who began teaching biology at Ursuline in 1968, recalled that enrollment had skyrocketed since his graduation in the mid-1950s. "In 1960, there were about 1,300 students enrolled at Ursuline," he explained. "By 1963, there were more than 1,700 students. When I arrived as an instructor in 1968, you had three students sharing a single locker."[156]

Meanwhile, Father Richard Murphy, who enrolled at the high school in the fall of 1969, was struck by the fact that Ursuline had twenty-four nuns on its faculty, along with ten priests, at a time when religious instructors were disappearing from parish schools. "It was quite a religious atmosphere, and enrollment was at its peak," he stated. "When I came to Ursuline from junior high school, I had a sense that this was a city contained within a campus. It was that vital."[157]

Father Murphy, who is the current president of Ursuline High School, described the excitement surrounding the annual Ursuline-Mooney football game, a celebrated local sports event. "There was always a huge crowd gathered for the bonfire, which took place in a field next to the Arts Building," he recalled. "In the 1960s, there were at least 100 kids in the band, so they were just a powerful musical ensemble....The culture was appealing from the start."

He stressed, however, that while Ursuline was known for its esprit de corps, the school was also respected for its rigorous academic standards. "You didn't just read material and forget about it," Father Murphy insisted. "You had to read, write, interpret, evaluate, and judge—what are often called the higher thinking skills." He assumed most students took for granted the presence of so many Ursuline nuns on the school's faculty. "We didn't have a direct experience of St. Angela Merici or the origins of their charism," he acknowledged. "But we knew we were dealing with committed educators."

Standouts in the faculty included Sister Janet Frantz, a dedicated English instructor, and Sister Nancy Dawson, an enthusiastic and supportive teacher who was engaged in television work through the diocese. Students involved in WFMJ's weekly television show *Movin' Out* assisted Sister Nancy in the areas of production and writing, while also serving as news anchors and performing in skits. Father Murphy suggested that his participation in the youth television workshop helped him develop confidence as a public speaker.[158]

At the time, Ursuline High School was also a hotbed of religious reform. Sister Isabel Rudge recalled that her first few years at Ursuline High School coincided with the opening of Vatican II, and the school's auditorium, with its central location, became a popular venue for speakers on topics related to the council. She sensed that most members of the high school's faculty and administration were supportive of the council's reforms. "I was living in an atmosphere where people thought Vatican II was wonderful," she explained. "Therefore, I missed some of the negativity."[159]

However, more conservative members of the faculty, including John Ulicney, remembered things differently. At the time, Ulicney expressed ambivalence about some of the conciliar reforms. While he came to accept many of the changes that occurred within the church, the instructor was hardly alone in his initial discomfort.

For many Catholics in the United States, the most tangible symbol of change during the post-conciliar era was the vernacular mass, introduced in churches across the country on the first Sunday of Advent in 1964. While the impact of the liturgical changes is often downplayed, Mark S. Massa, SJ, has argued that the new liturgy "helped to shape new cultural nuances of 'being Catholic' in America."

Along with the social encyclicals of John XXIII, the introduction of the new mass contributed to a situation in which "American Catholics could now be labeled as 'liberal' or 'conservative'…based on (among other things) their reception of the mandated liturgical changes."[160]

In other contexts, changes that some observers dismissed as superficial became ideological lightning rods. When religious communities transitioned out of the formal habit, for instance, a similar rule of thumb was often applied to those nuns who doffed the veil and those who chose to retain it. This was equally true of those sisters who held onto their traditional religious names and those who reclaimed their baptismal names.

Over the next few years, Catholics in the United States would find themselves further divided over polarizing social and political issues that included the Vietnam War, the civil rights movement and the so-called sexual revolution. If the early 1960s struck many observers as an almost seamless continuation of the 1950s, it was apparent to everyone by the end of the decade that the country was radically different.

American youth, many of whom were shocked and dispirited by the assassination of President Kennedy, soon found themselves enraged by the overseas policies of his successor, President Lyndon B. Johnson, whose dramatic escalation of U.S. military involvement in Vietnam was criticized by members of his own party—notably Catholic politicians like Eugene McCarthy and Robert F. Kennedy—as illegal and unjust. "The president of the United States was suddenly a figure of disdain and mockery," observed news anchor Lawrence O'Donnell. "An alien exotic bohemia in political opposition to, it seemed, America itself had somehow zoomed in out of somewhere and invaded suburbia."[161]

Pessimism over the state of the union deepened after the back-to-back assassinations of civil rights leader Dr. Martin Luther King Jr. and presidential hopeful Robert Kennedy, which accelerated already unprecedented levels of civil unrest.

A rise in antiestablishment sentiment, which most likely influenced the exodus of young men and women from seminaries and convents, also fueled a generational divide within the Ursuline religious community, as many

Sister Patricia McNicholas works with a hearing-impaired child in the 1960s. *Courtesy of Ursuline Sisters of Youngstown/Vindicator Printing Co.*

older nuns sought to shore up traditional models of Catholic education, while younger sisters often struggled to make the church's teaching relevant to young people. In this uncertain atmosphere, religious education at some Catholic schools was transformed.

As early as the 1960s, parents accustomed to "a traditional presentation" began to criticize some of the religious textbooks used in parish and diocesan schools. Harold Buetow, writing in 1970, pointed out that such "complaints had similar patterns: pictures of the Rev. Martin Luther King, modern art illustrations, 'political' issues included in the text, the recommendation of folk songs by Pete Seeger, and a de-emphasis of the question-and-answer approach."[162]

This trend was reflected at Ursuline High School, where students were assigned readings from *The Electric Bible*, a textbook by Father John A. Swartz that used popular culture to shed light on the major themes of the Gospel. This contemporary approach to religious education was certain to annoy parents who preferred the old certainties of the *Baltimore Catechism*.

Debates regarding the content of religious textbooks were informed by disagreements over issues ranging from racial inequality to birth control. If some conservative Catholics were offended when Dr. King received an audience with Pope Paul VI in April 1964, their liberal counterparts were stunned by the pope's issuance, in July 1968, of "*Humanae Vitae*," an encyclical letter that upheld the church's ban on "artificial" birth control. Released only two years after a papal commission found no justification to continue the ban, "*Humanae Vitae*" is sometimes described as "the Vietnam War of the Catholic Church."[163]

A growing list of ideological divisions unavoidably affected Catholic schools, as more U.S. Catholics began to debate the purpose and content of religious education.

Yet by the late 1960s, a more direct threat to institutions like Ursuline High School was the relentless decline of urban neighborhoods that once sustained traditional "feeder schools." Examples of such schools included Saint Columba and Immaculate Conception, traditionally staffed by the Ursulines, and Saint Edward, which was staffed by the Sisters of the Humility of Mary.

In an ironic twist, some projects presented as efforts to "revitalize" the city accelerated the flow of people into the suburbs. Throughout the decade, Youngstown, like many other American cities, launched highway construction and urban renewal programs that targeted older residential areas.

One of the earliest casualties of planned highway construction was Saint Ann Parish and School, a landmark of the Brier Hill district on the city's north side. In 1960, the large, Norman-style parish complex was closed and pulled down to make way for the extension of a nearby expressway.[164]

Former parishioner Mary Rita (McNicholas) Carney, who referred to the incident as "Black '60," lamented the fact that the city razed her beloved parish to "build a highway that was never built." "The church was beautiful," she said. "I still have images of it in my wedding album, of course, and in my brain."[165]

Not long after the closure of Saint Ann Parish, highway construction on the city's south side involved the destruction of whole neighborhoods surrounding Saint Patrick School. The impact of this project, in combination with other trends, proved dramatic. Between 1960 and 1967, enrollment at the school fell from 1,057 to 615, reflecting a loss of about 40 percent of the student body.

Hence, few were surprised when the parish announced the closure of its junior high school annex, Saint Patrick Glenmary, which had been built in 1955 to accommodate a postwar spike in enrollment.[166]

Around the same time, the northward expansion of Youngstown State University imperiled longstanding neighborhoods on the city's lower north side, and in 1967, the growth of the university contributed to the closure of Saint Joseph Parish and School, a north side institution since 1874.[167] These developments would also take a toll on enrollment at Saint Columba School, which Ursuline nuns had staffed since 1874.

Meanwhile, highway construction resulted in the removal of the formerly stable Irish and Italian American enclaves surrounding Immaculate Conception Parish and School on the city's east side.[168] The combined effect of highway construction and urban renewal projects continued to plague heavily Catholic center city neighborhoods over the next decade.

While the city, at that point, still retained a relatively vibrant pattern of parish schools and hosted scores of working-class neighborhoods, it was becoming clear that the future would look much different—and the Ursulines would need to adjust their mission accordingly.

EXPANDING HORIZONS

By the early 1970s, the neighborhood around Immaculate Conception School was almost unrecognizable to those who came up on Youngstown's east side several decades earlier. Middle-aged residents of the district recalled a tight-knit, largely Italian American neighborhood that supported a slew of family-owned businesses, including Montella's Isaly's Store, McNally's Candy Store, Scarsella's Furniture and DeMain's Royal Oaks Tavern.

Dozens of parishioners lived within walking distance of Immaculate Conception Church, and students at the parish school often returned to their homes in the early afternoon to eat lunch.

All that changed with the construction of an interstate highway that practically bisected the district, wiping out blocks of housing and accelerating a decline in the parish's congregation.[169] Between the late 1960s and 1970s, Immaculate Conception's membership plummeted from 1,500 to 700.[170]

At the same time, the area around the parish, which had become an Italian American enclave by the 1950s, was rapidly hollowing out as more established residents pulled up stakes and moved to outlying communities. Most of the district's newer residents were poorer than their predecessors had been.

This became obvious to Sister Teresa Winsen in 1969, when she was transferred from the south side parish school of Saint Patrick to Immaculate Conception School. Indeed, the new principal was startled by the differences she observed between the two institutions.[171]

In the late 1950s, Immaculate Conception Parish was the centerpiece of a vibrant working-class neighborhood that fell victim to a combination of postwar urban trends. *Courtesy of Benjamin J. Lariccia.*

At Immaculate Conception, endemic poverty—combined with demographic changes that reduced the number of Catholic residents—fueled a trend toward declining enrollment. As the decade concluded, it was difficult to imagine that as recently as September 1960, the parish school had opened with a peak enrollment of 693 students. By the time Sister Teresa's arrived, enrollment had slipped to a meager 411 students.[172]

These challenges were eventually exacerbated by rising operational costs in diocesan schools. At this stage, teachers' salaries were probably a minor factor in the school's rising expenses, as most lay instructors were parishioners who received modest compensation for their services. As a rule, lay teachers at schools like Immaculate Conception were paid little more than their religious counterparts, whose salaries were practically stipends.

Still, the growing percentage of lay teachers ensured that expenses related to the payment of instructors would continue to rise, given that salary increases at diocesan secondary schools heightened pressure on parish schools to boost their teachers' annual salaries. As the *Vindicator* reported in 1969, diocesan high schools were paying lay teachers "95 percent of the public high school salary schedule."

The same article noted that the modest annual salaries of teaching nuns would increase over the next three years, rising from $1,800 in September 1969 to $2,500 in September 1971.[173] The astonishingly low rate of pay afforded religious instructors underscored the relevance of a growing trend in Catholic elementary and secondary schools: an increase in the number and percentage of lay instructors.[174]

As Sister Charlotte Italiano pointed out in an interview, "The success of the Catholic school system in the United States…was on the backs of the nuns."[175] This is hardly an exaggeration. According to a 1952 survey conducted by the National Catholic Education Association (NCEA), 45 percent of participating religious communities reported "that the cost of supporting a sister at a basic level exceeded the amount of her teaching stipend."

A careful examination of this figure reveals that many religious communities "were subsidizing Catholic school systems rather than the other way around."[176] Thus, it should come as no surprise that the arrival into the classroom of large numbers of lay teachers in need of greater remuneration placed a strain on parish schools.

In 1970, Sister Mary Conroy, who served on the faculty at Youngstown State University, drew a correlation between declining religious instructors in the classroom and rising parochial school operational expenses. She noted that diocesan school salaries, which totaled $917,000 in 1965, had risen to $1,882,000 in 1970. Sister Mary attributed this increase mainly to the fact that a growing number of lay teachers received "95 per cent of the scale paid public school teachers in the district where the Catholic high schools are located."[177]

Given that the Diocese of Youngstown was unprepared to provide much in the way of supplemental funding to beleaguered urban parish schools, the principals of these institutions were forced to employ unconventional strategies—including citywide fundraising efforts and grant-writing campaigns—to maintain operations. A few of these institutions were also taking steps to ensure that educational services were available to underprivileged children in the surrounding neighborhood, many of whom had no connection to the parish.

Sister Teresa had few rivals in the areas of fundraising and community outreach. Apart from raising money to establish a school scholarship fund, she visited homes to get a better picture of the challenges facing the east side's poor families. "As an administrator, I found it necessary to provide donations and services to the poorer families in the area," Sister Teresa explained. "To get an idea of the poverty that existed among those families,

I really needed to visit the homes." She was shocked at the level of material deprivation she encountered in some households. "I remember visiting one home, and the children said to me, 'We have no food,'" she recalled. "Well, I couldn't believe that, so I said, 'Let's look in the cupboard,' and there was nothing—absolutely nothing. I returned to the school and collected extra lunches for these children."

Throughout this period, Sister Teresa's administration took an active interest in the surrounding neighborhood. At the beginning of 1970, the parish school even became involved in municipal politics when Sister Teresa helped put a spotlight on the east side's substandard infrastructure. Visits to students' homes brought her face to face with problems that required the city's intervention.

The principal recalled entering one home in which "there were no water lines and no lavatories." When she asked about a restroom, a resident "showed me a room with several buckets." With a sense of urgency, Sister Teresa alerted Youngstown mayor Jack C. Hunter and city council about the need to install sewer lines in some of the impoverished neighborhoods around Immaculate Conception Parish.[178]

The *Vindicator* reported that the school principal "made a personal investigation of conditions in the area and found them appalling." Sister Teresa explained that she encountered "some occupied homes without toilet facilities of any type, others with defective septic tanks, and some without water, sewers, or toilet facilities."[179]

Looking back, Sister Teresa praised municipal leaders for their response in language that reflected her commitment to the neighborhood.

Her first opportunity to alert the city to conditions in portions of the east side came when Second Ward councilman Peter "Pete" Starks, a leader within the local Black community, invited her to speak before a caucus of the Youngstown City Council. "When I begged for sewer lines and water lines on the east side, the municipal government listened," she recalled. "We had to be the advocates and voice for the poor."

Strangely, most of the homes in question had been built a few years earlier. For reasons that remain unclear, these newer homes were constructed in areas that lacked access to existing water lines, and no attempt had been made to extend water lines to those neighborhoods. The east side residents who lived in these homes were overwhelmingly poor, and most were Black.[180] Due largely to Sister Teresa's efforts, these conditions were exposed through the local media.

Sister Darla Jean Vogelsang, who taught at Immaculate Conception during this time, engaged in the kind of neighborhood outreach Sister

Teresa encouraged. "We did a lot, and we saw a lot," she said. "We had kids who would come to school with impetigo [a contagious skin disease], and when we visited the home, we found they were living in the basement of a house that had a dirt floor."

She confirmed that Sister Teresa was adamant about the importance of visiting students' homes. "We were always able to identify the poverty that [the students] were coming out of," she explained. Sister Darla Jean noted that when Ursuline Sisters entered the homes of impoverished students with food items, desperate children occasionally grabbed packages of meat from their arms and started "eating raw hamburger."[181]

As the decade progressed, Immaculate Conception and its south side neighbor, Saint Patrick, were categorized as *inner-city* parochial schools, a term that revealed less about these institutions' locations than it did about the demographic characteristics of their surrounding neighborhoods.

Over time, the term *inner-city* was applied to more urban parish schools as they began to show qualities already evident at institutions like Immaculate Conception School. These characteristics included declining parish contributions, rising numbers of low-income neighbors and a larger percentage of non-Catholic students.

As early as 1972, many parish schools in Youngstown's oldest neighborhoods were battling for survival. In the spring of that year, the city's premier parish school, Saint Columba, was forced to close its doors when the surrounding residential area was destroyed by a variety of urban renewal projects. In the late 1960s and early 1970s, large sections of the neighborhood north of Youngstown State University were razed to accommodate projects including the construction of Interstate 680, an urban beltway that was built as part of the national interstate highway development program.

As Sherry Linkon and John Russo wrote in *Steeltown U.S.A.*, "The promised residential and commercial development resulting from the construction of I-680 never materialized, but the suburbs boomed." Indeed, the highway project virtually isolated the city's traditional center, "directing drivers, and more important, shoppers to the new strip malls" that had arisen to the north and south of downtown Youngstown.[182]

Local Catholic leaders, apparently hesitant to criticize popular public works projects, downplayed the effect of urban renewal on Catholic institutions. Diocesan officials assured local Catholics that the needs of students affected by the school's closure would be addressed, and they announced Saint Columba would be consolidated with Immaculate Conception and Saint Edward Elementary Schools.

Sister Mary Dunn directs students in a cleanup operation near Saint Patrick School in 1978. *Courtesy of Saint Patrick Parish/Vindicator Printing Co.*

These officials probably understood that the problem of declining enrollment was not restricted to Youngstown's center city. A newspaper article on the consolidation of Saint Columba with two other parish schools pointed out that enrollment among all schools of the six-county diocese was dropping "because of a declining birth rate and tuition costs."[183] For center city parishes, however, these trends intersected with sweeping demographic changes—and the unintended consequences of urban renewal—to produce severe economic challenges.

LENDING SUPPORT TO OTHER RELIGIOUS COMMUNITIES

Amid the dislocations of the 1970s, the Ursuline Sisters of Youngstown moved away from the kind of organizational insularity that worked against meaningful cooperation with sister communities. As early as the 1960s, with the establishment of the new motherhouse, the Ursulines opened their educational program to the Oblate Sisters of the Sacred Heart of Jesus, an Italian religious community that settled in the Mahoning Valley after World War II.

By the end of the 1960s, they had also initiated what would become a long and fruitful relationship with the Antonine Sisters, a Maronite (Eastern Rite) community that established a local presence. The group's arrival in the area coincided with the construction of the Basilica and National Shrine of Our Lady of Lebanon in nearby North Jackson, Ohio. Notably, the shrine was a $200,000 stone replica of a considerably larger monument in Harissa, Lebanon.

The driving force behind the project, Monsignor Peter Eid, the pastor of Saint Maron Parish in Youngstown, reached out to a group of Antonine Sisters who were then studying with the Ursuline Sisters of Cleveland. In 1965, the year of the shrine's completion, he invited them to build a community in North Jackson. "When the sisters finished their studies in Cleveland, they agreed to relocate to the shrine," explained Sister Marie Madeleine Iskander, Religious of the Assumption (RA), who arrived in Northeast Ohio a few years later.

The product of a large and deeply religious family in Northern Lebanon, Sister Marie Madeleine spoke Arabic and French but no English when she began her studies in the United States. To accelerate her acquisition of English language skills, leaders of her Antonine community sent Sister Marie Madeleine to live with a small group of Ursuline Sisters who were based at Saint Rose Parish in Girard.

During her months at the parish convent, Sister Marie Madeleine formed close bonds with members of the Ursuline community, including Sister Mary Ann Diersing and Sister Eleanor Santangelo. "Some of the Ursulines I lived with have since died or left the community, but all of them were so kind and patient with me as I struggled to improve my English," she recalled.

The young nun thrived in the welcoming atmosphere of the Ursuline community at Saint Rose Parish. Within a few months, Sister Marie Madeleine attained enough fluency to begin her studies with the Ursuline Sisters of Cleveland. "I stayed [in Cleveland] for two years, where I finished

During the 1970s, the religious teaching staff at Saint Rose School hosted Sister Marie Madeleine Iskander (*seated on floor, far right*), an Antonine nun from Lebanon. Standing (*left to right*) are Sister Helen Therese Tesner, Sister Eleanor Santangelo, Sister Justin (Regina Olivia) and Sister Mary Ann Diersing. In the second row (*left to right*) are Sister Therese Ann Rich, Sister Andrea Pernotto, Sister Rachel (Nancy Hortzman) and Sister Nancy Pawlen. Sitting on the floor (*left*) is Sister Thecla (Mary Glasser). *Courtesy of Ursuline Sisters of Youngstown.*

my BA," she explained. "Then I went to Chicago to finish my degrees at Loyola University."

Over time, the Antonine community's relationship with the Ursuline Sisters of Youngstown deepened. "Starting in 1974, they taught us an awful lot, because we were not accustomed to how things work in the United States," Sister Mary Madeleine observed. "To this day, if we want to organize a retreat, we go to the Ursuline Motherhouse. If one of our sisters needs to study and requires time away from our community, we send them to stay with the Ursulines in either Youngstown or Cleveland."

The Ursulines' support proved critical two decades later, when the Antonine Sisters expanded their ministry. Sister Marie Madeleine explained that during the 1990s, when the community moved forward with plans to establish an adult daycare center in North Jackson, the Ursulines offered both guidance and material support. "When we started this project, we didn't have any money," she noted. "So, I approached Sr. Patricia [McNicholas], who was then general superior, and asked if the Ursulines could help us to build this house—and they agreed."

The Ursuline Sisters not only provided a no-interest loan for the project but also advised the Antonine Sisters to seek the support of such organizations as the Sisters of Humility of Mary and Catholic Charities. The project eventually won the influential support of Youngstown bishop James Malone, who had been aware of the need for such a facility in the diocese.

When it became clear that the prospective daycare center would be obligated to provide medical care to senior clients, Sister Jeanne Cigolle, an Ursuline nun and registered nurse, offered to serve as a consultant. Sister Jeanne later became the facility's in-house nurse, maintaining an office there for more than a decade. "Today, we have buses that pick up the seniors every morning, and we take care of them until the afternoon," explained Sister Marie Madeleine, who, as of this writing, serves as the center's director. "None of this would have happened without the help of the Ursulines. When you imagine the Antonine and Ursuline Sisters, you need to think of us as one family."[184]

Over time, the Ursulines' cooperation with other religious communities enabled them to pool their talents and resources in ways that enhanced their positive impact on the surrounding community.

A Community in Transition Marks Its Centennial

On the afternoon of November 24, 1974, the Ursuline Sisters of Youngstown marked their community's centennial during a mass of thanksgiving held at Saint Columba Cathedral. An article in the *Youngstown Vindicator* announcing the service indicated that the religious community's "influence, example and dedication have left indelible imprints on the minds and hearts of a large section of the community."

The mass, led by Youngstown bishop James Malone, was celebrated more than two months after the Ursulines' official centennial on September 18, 1974. Sister Mary Ellen Dean and Sister Jerome Corcoran had already prepared for the milestone by producing a centennial booklet that included an overview of the community's rich history in the Mahoning Valley.[185] In their joint text, they acknowledged that "[m]yriad changes have occurred in the dwellings, the dress, and the lives of the Ursulines since 1874."[186]

The Ursuline Sisters who were on hand for the centennial service had experienced many of these changes firsthand. Among those in attendance was Sister Darla Jean Vogelsang, who had entered the novitiate in 1960 as a seventeen-year-old graduate of Ursuline High School. Dazzled by the charms of the old motherhouse on Logan Avenue, she said she would never forget her first glimpse of the elegant chapel with its "gorgeous" oval doors that opened onto the lush grounds of the former estate. "It was hard to let go of 'Logan' because it was such a beautiful historic building," Sister Darla Jean recalled.

A few years later, Sister Darla Jean's class of forty-five novices was excited to learn that their clothing ceremony at Saint Columba Cathedral would be aired on a local television station. "It was televised live all over the city," she explained.

Yet within a little more than a decade, the community's clothing ceremony had become a relic of the past. By the late 1970s, the name of the entrance rite for novices was officially changed from *clothing* to *reception*, a reflection of the religious habit's decreasing importance. "After 1964, we started working on the document of renewal on consecrated life," Sister Darla Jean explained. "That resulted in the change in habit. We went from those gimps…to capes and then black suits with a smaller veil. I went through it all."

Over time, a growing number of sisters chose to doff the veil, and most members of the community underwent a name change. "We went back to our baptismal names," Sister Darla Jean noted. "I was clothed as Sr. Mary Benedict, and we were allowed to go back to our baptismal names at that time."

These developments coincided with an even stronger emphasis on education, which had been a hallmark of the Ursulines for decades. "We were often educated by our own nuns, but we graduated from Youngstown University," Sister Darla Jean recalled. "The first time I set foot on campus was when I graduated.…I never went to one class there because we were taught by the nuns at the motherhouse."[187]

Sister Mary Alyce Koval, who entered the community in 1965, shortly after graduating from Ursuline High School, described a similar focus on academic credentials. She indicated the first floor of the new motherhouse in Canfield was mainly reserved for classrooms, some of which were staffed by professors from then Youngstown University. "It became Youngstown State University…when I was a senior in college," she recalled. Thereafter, members of the community took classes on YSU's campus.

Like many young women who were drawn to the Ursulines in the 1960s, Sister Mary Alyce was impressed by the group's commitment to education.

Her introduction to the Ursulines as teachers occurred when she was a student at Saints Peter and Paul School, which sat a few blocks northwest of downtown Youngstown. "I had Ursuline Sisters in first grade, second grade, fifth, sixth, seventh and eighth grades," she explained. "They influenced me and supported me in everything."

She shared fond memories of Sister Bernice Bosanac, the school's principal, and Sister Marie Antoinette Shipka, the politically engaged daughter of a local labor leader. "I had Sr. Marie Antoinette in eighth grade, when President Kennedy was elected," she recalled. "We followed that whole election process, and we were counting electoral votes....To this day, every time we have an election, I think of her."

Over time, Sister Mary Alyce's maternal aunt Sister Mary Volk introduced her to many of the nuns who taught at Ursuline High School. When she enrolled at the school in the early 1960s, she came under the influence of dedicated instructors like Sister Alice Marie Morley and Sister Marcia Welsh. In the end, however, it was Sister Gertrude Paris, a former teacher at Saints Peter and Paul School, who encouraged her to consider a vocation. "[Sister Gertrude] was the first one that ever asked me, 'Mary Alyce, did you ever think about becoming a nun?'" she recalled.

Like many Ursuline Sisters, Sister Mary Alyce spent decades as an educator, teaching at such elementary schools as Saint Nicholas (Struthers), Saint Rose (Girard) and Saint Luke (Boardman); she also later served as the principal at Saint Joseph (Austintown), Saint Rose (Girard) and Saint Charles (Boardman). Years later, however, she was drawn to ministries outside formal education.[188]

Notably, in 1977, a discussion was initiated on whether the Ursulines should continue serving primarily as educators. As one institutional history observed, these conversations fueled uneasiness among some sisters who had already taken the fourth vow to engage in the instruction of youth.

The community reached an impasse during its 1977 chapter meeting. "The discussions became so intense that the moderator suggested that the Chapter be adjourned for several hours to permit everyone time for discernment," the document continued. "When the Chapter re-adjourned in the afternoon, the discussions included a look at how the Vow Formula had already changed several times over the years." The sisters also debated how the order "would define ministry in light of Angela's directive 'to adjust our ministries according to the signs of the times.'"[189] Finally, in its interim constitution of 1979, the community arrived at the following compromise:

Ursuline Sisters, who have taken a Vow of Instruction, shall willingly accept the duty of teaching; however, the principle of diversity is accepted. Sisters appointed to other offices or charges will fulfill their obligation of the Vow of Instruction by faithfully accepting and performing their appointed duties, all of which contribute at least indirectly to the apostolate of education. Because the person is of prime value, the choice of apostolic work is the joint concern of each Sister and the Community, taking cognizance of her individual charism, talents, capabilities, and desires, as well as the needs of the Church and the commitments of the Community in response to those needs.[190]

Sister Isabel Rudge evidently anticipated this compromise when she considered alternatives to teaching in 1977. The veteran educator was then in her fifth year as an administrative assistant at Ursuline High School, where she had already spent thirteen years teaching and two years serving as an office worker. While she was comfortable working at the high school, Sister Isabel sensed a need for a change.

Her transition to a new ministry began with an unexpected phone call from an old friend, Sister Mary Conroy, who had served as the general superior between 1972 and 1976. Sister Mary asked Sister Isabel if she ever considered working at the Diocesan Marriage Tribunal. She added that Bishop James Malone wanted someone to "take over" as office manager and advocate for the people at the Diocesan Marriage Tribunal, which dealt with such issues as annulment. While the position did not specifically require a degree in canon law, candidates were expected to have "common sense."

Sister Mary urged Sister Isabel to schedule an appointment with Auxiliary Bishop William Hughes, who agreed to meet with her. During that meeting, Bishop Hughes explained to Sister Isabel that American procedural norms in canon law had changed to permit the introduction of new grounds to prove that a marriage was invalid. However, these reforms had been roundly rejected by the diocese's canonist, an elderly priest who was scheduled to retire several months later.

Before accepting the position, Sister Isabel consulted with longtime friends Sister LaVerne Weinheimer, Sister Nancy Dawson and Monsignor Robert Fannon, the pastor of Saint Rose Parish in Girard. At one point, Monsignor Fannon dolefully informed her that the new procedures were already in place in the Diocese of Cleveland. Aware of the situation's gravity, Sister Isabel scheduled another meeting with Bishop Hughes and agreed to take the job.

In the 1970s, Sister Mary Ann Coz served as the founding director of the Diocesan Media Library. *Courtesy of Ursuline Sisters of Youngstown.*

While she was energized by her new role at the Diocesan Marriage Tribunal, Sister Isabel was unsettled by a conversation involving another member of her religious community, who asked, "Are you sure you're keeping your vows by working where you're working?" Sister Isabel was stunned by the question. "All I could think was…St. Angela Merici would work in the tribunal if she were alive," she recalled.[191]

Sister Isabel's tenure at the Diocesan Marriage Tribunal coincided with a period in which more Ursuline Sisters were choosing to step back from duties at parish and diocesan schools. Hence, when she agreed to accept the position at the tribunal in the late 1970s, she joined an expanding group of Ursulines whose influence extended across the diocese.

At the time, Sister Rita DeChello served as the director of Pupil Personnel Services (an office dedicated to adapting education to the needs of students). Meanwhile, Sister Mary Ann Coz was the director of the Diocesan Media Library, Sister Patricia McNicholas served as the director of Catechist Formation and Certification and Sister Mary Conroy led the Religious Education Department in Stark County. Sister Mary eventually earned a license in canon law from the Catholic University of America and became the first woman to serve as a canon lawyer for the tribunal.

The May 1980 dedication of George Segal's sculpture *The Steelworkers* coincided with the collapse of the Mahoning Valley's steel industry. The sculpture currently stands on the grounds of the Youngstown Historical Center of Industry and Labor. *Courtesy of Thomas Welsh.*

Similarly, Sister Elizabeth Kerrigan functioned as vicar for the religious, while Sister Nancy Dawson was concluding her third and final year at the Diocesan Communication Department.[192]

Eventually, at least seventeen nuns, including Sister Isabel, would participate in the community's healthcare ministry. The others were Sister Jeanne Cigolle, Sister Mary Ann Diersing, Sister Shirley Getz, Sister Marilyn Hoover, Sister Marie Hughes, Sister Dorothy Kundracik, Sister Marie Maravola, Sister Virginia McDermott, Sister Kathleen Minchin, Sister Helen Nordick, Sister Brendan Sherlock, Sister Judy Shoff, Sister Diane Toth, Sister Darla Jean Vogelsang, Sister Lois Walter and Sister Marcia Welsh.[193]

A rising number of sisters also began to pursue opportunities as directors of religious education at diocesan parishes, while more pastors came to recognize that these women possessed the skills needed to create these positions. Sister Isabel indicated critics of this trend believed the Ursulines were giving everything up when they stepped back from their longstanding role as educators.[194]

Such trends became more pronounced as the Mahoning Valley's economic situation changed. A grim chapter in the community's history opened on September 19, 1977, when representatives of Youngstown Sheet and Tube Co. announced the closure of the company's huge facility in nearby Campbell, along with smaller plants in Struthers. The Campbell shutdown itself resulted in the loss of five thousand jobs in the Youngstown area and proved to be the first in a series of crippling economic developments.[195]

The shutdown of Youngstown Sheet and Tube Co.'s operations in Campbell and Struthers was followed by the staged withdrawal of U.S. Steel in 1979 and 1980, which resulted in the closure of massive steel plants in Youngstown and neighboring McDonald.[196] Another string of closings came with the bankruptcy of Republic Steel in the 1980s.

Thus, in several years, the Steel Valley—a onetime industrial zone comprising Mahoning and Trumbull Counties, as well as parts of western Pennsylvania—lost an estimated four hundred thousand manufacturing jobs, four hundred satellite businesses, $414 million in personal income and between 33 and 75 percent of its school tax revenues.[197]

Deindustrialization not only compounded trends that were already undermining Catholic schools but also exacerbated such growing concerns as economic disparity, racial inequality, domestic violence and poverty. As the project of Catholic education became increasingly difficult to sustain, the Ursuline Sisters of Youngstown were confronted with a new set of challenges that required their attention.

6

"WALKING THE WALK"

B y the early 1980s, despite the rather modest size of the Diocese of Youngstown, Bishop James Malone had emerged as a prominent figure in national religious affairs. Several years earlier, the bishop earned a measure of notoriety as an organizer of the Ecumenical Coalition of the Mahoning Valley, an activist group comprising church leaders and steelworkers who between 1977 and 1979 raised funds in a courageous—albeit doomed—effort to reopen the Campbell Works of the defunct Youngstown Sheet and Tube Co.[198]

With his unique combination of gifts, Bishop Malone's election as president of the U.S. National Council of Bishops in November 1983 was treated in the national media as a foregone conclusion. The *New York Times* noted that the bishop's peers "describe him as a quiet, progressive leader who stands firmly but not militantly on social issues."[199]

Despite his reputation for diplomacy, however, Bishop Malone soon found himself in disagreement with Pope John Paul II, who promoted a vision of the church that was strictly hierarchical, far removed from the post–Vatican II model, which envisioned the church as "the people of God." The pontiff appointed highly conservative bishops to the church's far-flung dioceses and "rarely engaged in serious consultation" with episcopal leaders.[200]

Progressives who were aware of the Vatican's conservative domestic policy became increasingly concerned about the rightward tilt in its foreign policy, as Pope John Paul II forged close ties with Western powers to undermine Soviet communism and curb communist influence in Latin America.[201] Some

In February 1980, the first edition of Ursuline High School's alumni magazine was reviewed by (*left to right*) Sister Rosemary Deibel, then Ursuline principal Thomas Carey (*standing*), Bishop James Malone and business leader William Lyden. *Reprinted from the* Vindicator @ *Vindicator Printing Co., 2023.*

observers complained that the pope's failure to identify with the victims of right-wing regimes in Latin America was inconsistent with his outspoken support for the Solidarity labor movement in his native Poland.[202]

Almost inevitably, Bishop Malone, who served as the president of the U.S. Conference of Catholic Bishops from 1983 to 1986, emerged as a vocal critic of the Vatican's policies. During his tenure, he took aim at the "prophets of gloom," who argued that the church could "be saved only by returning to some earlier, fictitious, golden age."[203]

Skeptical observers like Bishop Malone acknowledged Pope John Paul's global stature as a leader "who had shaken the foundations of the Soviet empire," but they feared his approach to internal leadership gave "new life to the old conservatism and only put off the day of reckoning with necessary changes that the Council had prefigured."[204]

By and large, the Ursuline Sisters of Youngstown, under the leadership of Sister Nancy Dawson, were uncomfortable with this conservative retrenchment. Sister Nancy, who had been elected as general superior in the spring of 1984, was joined by a high-powered group of councilors: Sister Isabel Rudge, a member of the diocesan tribunal and staff member of the permanent diaconate; Sister Patricia McNicholas, the diocesan director of religious education; Sister Martina Casey, the principal of Saint Charles School in Boardman; and Sister Mary Dunn, the principal of Youngstown's Saint Patrick School.

Each of these women had embraced the reforms of the Second Vatican Council and were unlikely to welcome the pre-conciliar clericalism promoted by the pope and his supporters. Moreover, in the wake of the groundbreaking social and political movements of the 1960s, they questioned the pope's apparent embrace of leaders who showed little concern about such issues as racial and economic inequality.

Under these conditions, the lines between morality and politics became increasingly ill-defined, and some Ursuline Sisters found themselves grappling with topics that were once considered too politically charged to address. This situation inspired the rise of new ministries and informed the direction of the Ursulines' longstanding commitment to education, even as they struggled with the realities of a dwindling community.

A Move Toward Social Justice

Among the first members of the Ursuline religious community to move in the direction of peace and social justice activism was Sister Marcia Welsh, a retired math instructor.

An unlikely candidate for this undertaking, Sister Marcia had taught mathematics for ten years at what was then Youngstown College before entering the Ursuline religious community in 1956. Her subsequent teaching career at Ursuline High School spanned almost two decades.

Years later, Sister Marcia explained that her engagement with social issues had been fostered by her late mother, Irene Hogan Welsh, an advocate of women's suffrage during her college years who eventually became an ardent admirer of Catholic activist Dorothy Day.[205]

After leaving the classroom, Sister Marcia's initial work as a pastoral educational specialist at local nursing homes attracted little attention. However, in the spring of 1984, she found herself in the local news when she became involved in Witness for Peace, an internationally recognized

Sister Marcia Welsh was one of a growing number of Ursuline Sisters who were addressing social issues in the 1980s. *Courtesy of Ursuline Sisters of Youngstown.*

peace program that challenged the U.S. government's policies in war-torn Nicaragua.

In June 1984, Sister Marcia joined other members of Witness for Peace, a group that represented thirteen denominations from forty-eight states, on a nine-day visit to the Nicaragua-Honduras border. The group's activities on the border, which included planting crops, had already succeeded in interrupting armed incursions by the U.S.-backed Contras, a paramilitary group dedicated to the overthrow of Nicaragua's revolutionary government.

According to the *Vindicator*, the members of Witness for Peace included "pastors, housewives, and delegates to the Democratic National Convention." In a public statement, the organization contended "that U.S. intervention in Nicaragua and elsewhere is contrary to the witness of Scripture and the best of American values of democracy."[206]

Upon her return to Youngstown that summer, Sister Marcia accepted an assignment in Washington, D.C., where she joined the staff of *Sojourners*, a national ecumenical periodical published by Christian activist Jim Wallis. In 1985, while active with Pax Christi Metro DC–Baltimore, an organization dedicated to nonviolent, faith-based activism, Sister Marcia was jailed twice for picketing outside the Embassy of South Africa. In retrospect, she concluded that this experience planted the seeds for her later commitment to prison ministry, because it raised questions in her mind about the use of penal institutions as warehouses.[207]

Meanwhile, Sister Marcia spent two years as an administrator for the Washington, D.C.–based nonprofit So Others May Eat (SOME), where she coordinated volunteers in a dining room that provided one thousand meals a day to the poor and homeless. Over the next six years, she served as the coordinator of Harvest House Senior Center, one of the fourteen sites established by SOME to address the needs of "the homeless, the aging, the working poor, single-parent families and those suffering from addictions."

Working with a staff of four, along with available volunteers, she oversaw programs to meet "the physical, spiritual, and social needs of senior citizens," some of whom lived in community residential facilities. "Here in Washington, I've been involved in a combination of ministries [that] I've felt called to during my years of teaching," Sister Marcia observed.[208] After eight years in the nation's capital, Sister Marcia returned to the Youngstown area, where she devoted her remaining active years to prison ministry.[209]

By the late 1980s, Sister Marcia was scarcely an outlier in a community that was visibly engaged with a range of social justice issues. In April 1986, less than two years after Sister Marcia's departure for Nicaragua, Sister Rose Dailey was appointed by the Ursuline Sisters to lead a full-time ministry dedicated to peace and justice issues, a role that involved cooperation with the American Friends Service Committee to promote nonviolence. "As a community we believe that the appointment of Sr. Rose to full-time ministry in educating for non-violence was in direct response by the Ursuline Sisters to the U.S. Bishops' Pastoral Letter on Peace," Sister Nancy stated. "And we are delighted to be able to work ecumenically."[210]

The *Vindicator* described Sister Rose's project Educating for Non-Violence as one "designed to provide information skills and tactics to people who wish to lead non-violent lives and make a positive contribution to building a peaceful environment in their homes, at work and in society."

Like most of her colleagues, Sister Rose devoted much of her previous career to teaching. As a director of religious education, she served at Saint Patrick's Church (Leetonia), Sacred Heart Church (Youngstown) and Saint Charles Church (Boardman). Meanwhile, she spent years as a classroom instructor at parish and diocesan schools, including Youngstown's Cardinal Mooney High School. While working with the adult education program of the Catholic Diocese of Youngstown, she taught classes at Walsh College (Canton).

Yet Sister Rose was hardly a newcomer to political activism. Her involvement in social justice causes can be traced back to the late 1970s, when she organized and served as Ursuline community chairman of a group known as the Social Concern Committee. In 1982, Sister Rose helped organize "a coast-to-coast march in support of the Farmer's Labor Organization of Cesar Chavez and worked the following summer with migrant farm workers from Colorado." She served as a key member of the Youngstown Coalition to Free South Africa, as well as the Youngstown Rainbow Coalition, an antiracist multicultural movement.

An active organizer of nonviolent demonstrations in Youngstown and elsewhere, Sister Rose participated in a peace march in New York City in 1982, along with the March for Jobs, Peace and Freedom in Washington, D.C., in 1984. By that time, she was also serving as a co-chair of the Youngstown Area Peace Council, a local nonprofit organization.[211]

Notably, an awareness of social justice issues was promoted even within the classrooms of parochial and diocesan schools. Brigid Kennedy, a former novice who currently serves as the chief mission officer of the Ursuline Sisters of Youngstown, explained that her initial exposure to political activism occurred when she was a student at Girard's Saint Rose School. "Sister Pauline Dalpe was my third-grade teacher," she noted. "I always tell people that she provided my first introduction to social justice."

During the late 1970s and early 1980s, Sister Pauline urged her students to participate in a letter-writing campaign aimed at an international food and drink processing conglomerate that was promoting the use of infant formula products in developing countries. The nun informed her class that what seemed like a benign business practice had produced devastating consequences. Sister Pauline explained that in the early 1970s, reports showed that the firm's promotion of dry milk formula at the expense of breastfeeding contributed to illness and infant deaths in impoverished countries. "I remember at eight thinking that we were going to change the world," Kennedy recalled.[212]

A Shrinking Footprint in Formal Education

The Ursuline Sisters' growing emphasis on social issues occurred at a time when members of the community were becoming less focused on classroom teaching. In February 1988, the *Vindicator* reported that more nuns were leaving classrooms in favor of other kinds of ministries.

Significantly, the exodus of Ursuline Sisters from local classrooms coincided with a sharp decline in membership within religious communities around the diocese. Sister Elizabeth Kerrigan, a diocesan vicar for the religious, indicated "retirement and death are taking their toll and fewer young women are joining the ranks."

Sister Nancy Pawlen, the principal of Boardman's Saint Charles Elementary School, sports a hat representing the Disney character Figment, a small purple dragon who says, "If you can dream it, you can do it." *Courtesy of Ursuline Sisters of Youngstown.*

Considering these trends, Sister Nancy Dawson suggested that a downsizing of the Catholic Church's once formidable infrastructure was inevitable. "Our institutions were built and staffed to respond to the needs of an immigrant church," Sister Nancy explained. "Today…religious [orders] with fewer, aging members and limited financial resources simply cannot afford to staff or own institutions." She quickly added that the Ursulines had "nurtured and trained competent lay teachers and administrators with Catholic, Christian values to replace us."[213]

Five years earlier, in 1983, Patricia McCabe Fleming became aware of this pattern when she accepted a position as assistant principal at Ursuline High School. At the time, she could not have predicted that her decision would result in a thirty-five-year commitment to the institution. Indeed, her tenure as the school's assistant principal would last until 1995, when she was appointed principal, a post she held until 2018.

Fleming had been no stranger to the Ursuline community, as she was a former student at Youngstown's St. Patrick and Struthers's Saint Nicholas

Schools, both of which were staffed by Ursuline Sisters. After enrolling at Cardinal Mooney High School in the early 1960s, she soon discovered that the Ursulines were among several teaching orders represented in the faculty—and they were known for their success at attracting vocations. "In that era, becoming a priest or nun was a viable option for young people," she noted. "There were many members of my class who entered the convent."

Yet by the early 1970s, many of those same young women had retreated from religious life to pursue careers, marriage or both. "Right now, the only one of my former classmates who remains a nun is Sister Norma Raupple," Fleming stated. "She's the only one left out of about nine or ten who entered the convent."

Later, as a parochial school educator, Fleming watched this trend play out in classrooms throughout the 1970s and early 1980s. After earning a bachelor's degree in English language and literature from Youngstown State University, she taught at Holy Name of Jesus School, which was connected to a Slovak American parish on Youngstown's west side.

While the school was gradually losing its religious faculty members, Fleming developed friendships with the Ursuline Sisters who continued to work there: Sister Janice Kusick, Sister Julia Baluch, Sister Mary Carmel Incarnato and Sister Mary William Yurko. In the end, what Mrs. Fleming envisioned as a temporary position evolved into a thirteen-year commitment, even though she eventually earned a master's degree in educational administration that positioned her for a career in secondary education. She formed a close bond with Sister Julia, a good-natured friend and mentor who introduced her to members of her religious community who were teaching at Ursuline High School.

In the summer of 1983, Fleming finally chose to apply for a position at Ursuline High School, where she was quickly hired as an assistant by then-principal Dr. Nick Wolsonovich. Two years later, when Dr. Wolsonovich was tapped as diocesan school superintendent, he was replaced by Father Daniel Venglarik, who became Fleming's close friend and advisor.

When Father Venglarik left the high school to become the pastor of Boardman's Saint Charles Parish in the mid-1990s, Fleming assumed the position of principal, while Sister Regina Rogers, a religious education instructor, succeeded her as the assistant principal. The two women soon developed a solid working relationship.

Fleming recalled that despite the shrinking percentage of nuns on the faculty, the Ursuline Sisters remained a vital presence at the school. "Sister Marlene LoGrasso and Sister Therese Ann Rich were on the teaching staff,

In 1984, the religious teaching staff at Ursuline High School included (*standing, left to right*) Sister Mary McCormick, Sister Ellen Rose Donovan, Sister Marie Celine Olejar, Sister Alice Marie Morley, Sister Mary Ellen Dean and then Sister Margaret Mary Minghetti. Seated (*from left to right*) are Sister Janet Elaine Walsh, Sister Jacqueline Herpy, Sister Eileen Kernan and Sister Marlene LoGrasso. *Courtesy of Ursuline Sisters of Youngstown.*

and Sister Julia was transferred to Ursuline a few years after I started to work there," Fleming noted. "Sr. Marie Celine Olejar served as the guidance counselor, and Sr. Alice Marie Morley was still teaching art there. Even though Sr. Rosemary Deibel had retired, she was still actively involved at the school."

During this time, Fleming was introduced to a new faculty member, Sister Mary McCormick, a youthful nun who, decades later, would lead the community as general superior. "Across campus stood the convent where the teaching nuns lived, along with Ursuline Sisters who were involved in other ministries, including parish work," she explained. "There must have been eighteen nuns living in that convent at that time."

Those nuns who lived on campus, regardless of whether they were faculty members, showed up regularly at religious services held in the school auditorium and joined in the excitement of sports rallies at the gymnasium. "Those were grand times," Fleming said. "But over the years, many of the sisters retired or went on to other ministries. Their numbers continued to dwindle, and eventually, no one was living in the convent. The building is still there, but it's used mainly for storage....It's really kind of sad."[214]

Sister Regina Rogers, who currently serves as a pastoral associate at Saint Edward Parish, linked the departure of nuns from classrooms to Vatican

II's overarching theme of social engagement. "That opened the door for other vocational opportunities," she observed. "That was the advantage, that people could move into something that…was a better fit for them."

At the same time, Sister Regina stressed, the Ursulines' vocational diversity reflected the rise of new social challenges. "One of the things we were called to do…in the wake of Vatican II, was to go back and examine our roots," she explained. "It's significant that Angela Merici herself was not a teacher. She met the need wherever she found the need."[215]

WELL-DESERVED TRIBUTES FOR DECADES OF SERVICE

Not surprisingly, as more teaching nuns approached retirement, the religious order's educational contributions gained a new level of recognition within the diocese. In August 1984, for instance, twelve Ursuline Sisters were honored at a special mass at Saint Columba Cathedral for their combined total of 485 years of service to the community.

Leading the list of honorees was Sister Rosemary Deibel, whose sixty-year career had included teaching assignments at the former Saint Columba and Sacred Heart Elementary Schools, as well as Ursuline High School, Walsh College (Canton) and Sister's College (Cleveland). During her lengthy tenure at Ursuline High School, Sister Rosemary had served as the assistant principal, dean of girls and director of forensics and drama. Her honors included the Diamond Award from the National Forensic League in recognition of her outstanding service to the Inter-Scholastic Speech Program.

Meanwhile, Sister Anne Marie Manley was honored for her fifty years of service that included teaching assignments at the former Saint Columba and Saint Ann schools, Saint John (Campbell), Saints Cyril and Methodius, Saint Nicholas (Struthers), Ursuline High School, Our Lady of Peace (Canton), Saint Patrick (Leetonia), Saint Rose (Girard) and Holy Family (Poland).

No less impressive were the achievements of the remaining nuns who marked their golden jubilees, including Sister Virginia McDermott, Sister Patrick McIlduff, Sister Madeleine McNally, Sister Victoria Pascarella and Sister Edith Weir. The five sisters who were marking silver jubilees comprised Sister Mary Dunn, Sister Dorothy Kundracik, Sister Mary Ann Diersing, Sister Elizabeth Anne Freidhoff and Sister Nancy Dawson.[216]

Less than a year later, in June 1985, honors were accorded to five other sisters who were marking fifty years with the Ursuline religious community:

During a December 1985 banquet, Father Daniel Venglarik, the principal of Ursuline High School, honored Sister Alice Marie Morley (*left*) and Sister Rosemary Deibel (*right*) for their contributions to the school's fine arts program. *Courtesy of the Diocese of Youngstown.*

Sister Mary Catherine Doran, Sister Marie Hughes, Sister Mary Agnes Convery, Sister Anne Lynch and Sister Jerome Corcoran, all of whom had joined the order as young women in February 1935. Amazingly, this small band of jubilarians contributed a combined total of 250 years of service to the community, primarily in the field of education.[217]

Given the length and scope of these women's careers, it was clear to even casual observers that the Ursuline Sisters of Youngstown had touched the lives of tens of thousands of area residents. Moreover, in recent years, their outreach had moved beyond the diocese's traditional constituents, as the mission of urban parochial schools was expanded to meet the needs of families in the surrounding neighborhoods, many of whom had no connection to the parishes that maintained those schools. This change reflected a significant departure from an older model of Catholic education that focused on the needs of the Catholic families who belonged to neighborhood parishes.

While the Ursulines' role in the maintenance of struggling urban parish schools was consistent with their commitment to meet the needs of the times, it coincided with a larger trend within the U.S. Catholic Church. During this period, in communities across the country, episcopal leaders actively supported the church's continued institutional presence in the

In 1989, Sister Miriam Engels and Sister Mary Dunn marked the seventy-fifth anniversary of Saint Patrick Parish with a small group of students. *Courtesy of Saint Patrick Parish (Youngstown)/Vindicator Printing Co.*

center city and voiced a commitment to the education of urban students, regardless of race or religion.[218]

By the late 1970s, two of Youngstown's urban parish schools—Saint Patrick and Immaculate Conception—served large numbers of non-Catholic students. In April 1977, the *Vindicator* reported that only 52 percent of the students at Saint Patrick School were Catholic, while about 60 percent were members of minority groups. Meanwhile, at Immaculate Conception, more than 43 percent of the students enrolled were not Catholic, and almost 38 percent belonged to minority groups.[219]

Consequently, even as the Ursuline Sisters became a less visible presence in Catholic schools, their educational impact on underprivileged populations grew considerably. This pattern was driven in part by urban families' disillusionment with public schools that evidently struck them as overcrowded and underfunded.

In October 1985, Michelle Cooper (*center*), the president of Saint Patrick Parish's Home and School Association, honored four of the school's principals, including (*left to right*) Sister Charlotte Italiano, Sister Miriam Engels, Sister Teresa Winsen and Sister Mary Dunn. *Courtesy of Saint Patrick Parish (Youngstown)/Vindicator Printing Co.*

Given that parish schools were increasingly perceived as anchors in declining urban neighborhoods, the religious educators who maintained these institutions drew greater recognition as the decade progressed.

In October 1985, for instance, Saint Patrick Home and School Association paid tribute to four principals whose leadership had enabled the parochial school to adapt to a flurry of often disruptive trends. In a ceremony held at the school, Michelle Cooper, the president of the home and school association, presented a gold-plated quartz desk clock to then-principal Sister Mary Dunn, who had served in that role since 1977.

The other honorees were former principals Sister Miriam Engels, who served from 1960 to 1963; Sister Teresa Winsen, who served from 1963 to 1969; and Sister Charlotte Italiano, who served from 1969 to 1977. (The late Sister Edna Marie Brindle, who led the school between 1945 and 1960, was honored posthumously.)[220]

Sister Jerome Corcoran's Ministry to the Poor

Yet not all educational outreach to low-income families was unfolding in the context of urban parish schools. By the late 1970s, trailblazers like Sister Jerome Corcoran had moved beyond the model of parochial education to address the educational needs of low-income preschool students, many of whom belonged to minority groups.

In 1976, Sister Jerome became the founder and executive director of Youngstown's Millcreek Children's Center (initially known as the Millcreek Child Development Center), a southside daycare facility on Glenwood Avenue that offered comprehensive education, health and nutrition services mainly to underprivileged families.

In a December 1986 interview with the *Vindicator*, the seventy-year-old nun argued that U.S. society was failing poor children "badly." Sister Jerome pointed out that the number of children living below the poverty line had risen by 10 percent since the late 1970s. "More than 50 percent of mothers with young children are working, usually at a service job—minimum or close to minimum wage with practically no benefits," she observed.[221]

From the outset, Sister Jerome's aptitude as an administrator was matched by her skills as a fundraiser, and her school benefited from the support of local, regional and national philanthropists. Among her more prominent patrons was Denise DeBartolo York, a business leader and philanthropist who also served as cochair of the San Francisco 49ers football team. "Sr. Jerome was incredible," she said. "I always thought of her as the Mother Teresa of Youngstown."

Over the years, York's connection to Sister Jerome moved beyond that of a patron. The two women developed a quasi-familial relationship, and York and her twin daughters, Jenna and Mara, routinely celebrated special occasions with the Ursuline nun. "On the girls' birthday we would bring two cakes to the Ursuline Motherhouse," she recalled.

That said, York indicated that her most cherished memories of Sister Jerome involved the Millcreek Children Center's annual preschool graduations. "When those little children got up on that stage and looked at Sr. Jerome, you could see the adoration in their eyes and the smiles on their faces," she explained. "I'd like to find some of those students who are still around, because she really saved a lot of souls."[222]

In 1993, with the help of wealthy donors like York, Sister Jerome opened a brand-new southside facility on the main artery of Market Street. Five years later, in 1998, Sister Jerome, along with Sister Mary Dunn and the board

Sister Jerome Corcoran, the executive director of the Millcreek Children's Center, greets children at the facility she established for low-income preschool students. *Courtesy of Ursuline Sisters of Youngstown.*

of a local nonprofit called Developing Potential Inc., opened a successful charter school known as Youngstown Community School.

Although Sister Jerome retired as the executive director of Millcreek Children's Center in 2012, when she was well into her nineties, she remained a tireless advocate of the underprivileged until her death in June 2021 at the age of 105.

Longtime friend and supporter Richard S. Scarsella pointed out that Sister Jerome's empathy for the underprivileged was complemented by her exceptional social and business skills. "People often forget that she had a doctorate, so she was operating at a higher level than most people," he explained. "She could hold her own with bankers and lawyers, and while she was utterly sincere, she was also shrewd and business savvy. When she fought for the needs of those who were less fortunate, she generally got what she wanted. Overall, the poor of the Mahoning Valley could not have benefited from a more dedicated champion."[223]

If a broad commitment to education remained central to the Ursuline Sisters' ministry during the 1980s, it was also clear that the order was moving in new and unexpected directions—a trend readily acknowledged by Youngstown bishop James Malone. In October 1985, Bishop Malone, while celebrating a mass to mark the 450th anniversary of the order's founding, pointed out that the Ursuline Sisters of Youngstown, apart from providing educational and pastoral services at twenty parishes, served in diocesan offices that focused on education, religious education, finance, church vocations and marriage issues.

Bishop Malone added that the community operated a school of music, a preschool and a range of tutorial and youth services programs while also serving "as chaplains and administrators in area hospitals and nursing homes, [facilitating] support groups at the Youngstown Hearing and Speech Center and [ministering] to the mentally handicapped and the minority poor."

The bishop praised the foresight of the community's founder, Saint Angela Merici, who had recommended "that fresh decisions be made with prudence in accordance with the times and the needs," making "it possible for Ursulines throughout the world to adapt to the communities in which they serve."[224]

This pattern was reflected in the success of the religious community's Merici Program, which focused on the needs of adults dealing with mental and behavioral health issues. Within a year of the order's anniversary celebration, the local Merici Program was providing social and religious services to fifty adults from sixteen parishes.[225]

Sustaining a Smaller Religious Community

Despite the rise of new ministries, challenges related to a shrinking religious community dominated Sister Nancy Dawson's agenda in 1984, when she was elected to the first of three six-year terms as the Ursulines' general superior.

Sister Nancy's predecessor, Sister Mary Conroy, who served the second of two terms between 1980 and 1984, had already taken steps to address the realities of declining membership. In 1983, for instance, Sister Mary had overseen the renovation of the original first-floor novitiate wing into administrative offices while converting another novitiate dormitory into bedrooms.

While Sister Nancy's election coincided with a period of uncertainty, her response to the news was informed by gratitude. "One of the greatest blessings in my life was when the sisters determined that I should be the leader of the community," she said.[226] These feelings of appreciation, however, soon gave way to a sense of urgency, as she recognized a need to further improve the community's motherhouse.

Sister Nancy determined that her first order of business as general superior would be to refurbish the facility's twenty-year-old chapel, which no longer met the spiritual or physical needs of the community. As a first step, she met with Sister Jerome Corcoran, who had worked with local architect Paul Ricciuti on the design of her school on Glenwood Avenue. Next, she obtained the services of the Youngstown-based architectural firm Buchanan, Ricciuti and Balog.

During the project's initial phase, Ricciuti consulted with David Van Galen, a colleague, to determine how much of the original chapel could be retained. Both architects were committed to preserving the integrity of architect P. Arthur D'Orazio's original design. After a careful review of the site, Ricciuti concluded that much of the original chapel could be preserved, including the exterior walls and stained-glass windows.

The architect learned that the community's chief concern about the current chapel was that "it conformed to the idea of a center aisle with seating on both sides and an altar in the middle." Drawing inspiration from the traditional rood screen, a partition that separated the chancel and nave in late medieval churches, Ricciuti and his collaborators reinvented the chapel's altar, creating a "centrally focused space" that was "defined in part by the use of oak screens of varying densities."

He explained that as worshippers progress toward the altar, they experience subtly different views of the sanctuary through the oak screens, which work together to "visually reduce the size of the worship area while allowing the unity of the entire space to remain intact." Ricciuti pointed out that the area in which the communion hosts are stored is now illuminated by a single beam of light.

When the architect and his colleagues introduced this element, they drew inspiration from the Holy of Holies, the inner sanctuary of the tabernacle that was a central element of the lost Temple of Jerusalem.

Meanwhile, the architectural firm removed the chapel's pews, a late feature of Christian liturgical architecture that did not become popular until the fifteenth century. "If you visit any major cathedral in Europe, there are no pews," Ricciuti observed. "They have chairs, instead."

This page: In 1984, the Ursuline Sisters set out to remodel the motherhouse's twenty-year-old chapel, which no longer met the needs of the community. *Courtesy of Ursuline Sisters of Youngstown.*

He stressed, however, that the decision to remove the pews was not wholly motivated by aesthetic considerations. The architectural firm was also determined to make the chapel more flexible and accessible, in keeping with the needs of an aging community. At the same time, the platform on which the communion table rested was redesigned to accommodate celebrants with mobility issues. A final element in the chapel's renovation was the installation of a new baptismal font.[227]

Sister Nancy's concerns extended beyond the chapel, however. She was compelled to address issues critical to the motherhouse's long-term viability. Assisting her in this task were members of the Century II Club, an outgrowth of the original Century Club, which had been organized in 1964 to help the order reduce its substantial building debt.

In a 1989 interview with the *Vindicator*, Joseph Vannuki, a member of the club's financial advisory committee, outlined improvements made during the 1988–89 fiscal year, "including water and gas lines, remodeling of the community room and Angela Auditorium, installation of smoke alarms, a new telephone system to replace one that was 25 years old, and emergency lighting."

Meanwhile, Sister Nancy highlighted the need for sanitary sewers and connections, pointing out "that the present septic tanks installed 25 years ago are no longer adequate." She indicated that she planned to meet with Mahoning County commissioners "to petition for sewer installation."

Sister Nancy also announced the imminent release of a site planning survey commissioned from the Cleveland-based accounting firm of Laventhol and Horwath, which would highlight "future needs such as development of the educational facility, health care center and other programs."[228]

In December 1988, as the Ursuline Sisters of Youngstown marked the twenty-fifth anniversary of the Ursuline Motherhouse, the refurbished chapel was the site of a special mass celebrated by Father Philip Rogers, the brother of Sister Regina Rogers.

In a public statement, Sister Nancy observed, "We are grateful for the past 25 years of celebrating life and ministry in this community and especially for the blessings we have in the dedicated lay people who have helped us make our mission possible."

Buried in the *Vindicator*'s feature article on the anniversary celebration, however, was a reference to the fact that only sixty-four Ursuline Sisters were then living in a motherhouse that was designed to accommodate more than one hundred nuns and novices.[229] While the community continued to encourage vocations, it had become evident that few young women were

Sister Bridget Nolan, as the assistant principal of Boardman's Saint Charles Elementary School, introduces a student during a variety show. *Courtesy of Ursuline Sisters of Youngstown.*

drawn to religious life, a pattern reflected in religious communities across the country.

This phenomenon, which raised serious questions about the future of the Ursuline Motherhouse, inspired Sister Nancy to lay the foundation for the facility's transformation into a multipurpose community center. Even as other religious communities maintained a business-as-usual posture in the face of the crisis brought on by declining vocations, the Ursuline Sisters of Youngstown were preparing for a future that was likely to be fraught with challenges.

PIONEERS IN MINISTRY

B y the end of the 1980s, the cumulative effect of declining vocations had taken its toll on the twenty-three religious communities active within the six-county Diocese of Youngstown. In February 1990, the *Vindicator* reported that between 1980 and 1989, the number of nuns in the diocese had fallen from 493 to 367. Furthermore, the average age of these sisters was about fifty-seven, which deepened concerns about the future of their respective religious communities.

Amid growing financial constraints, a handful of sisters resided in apartments, "because it is less costly than maintaining large convents," but the vast majority continued to live "in convents at parishes or [in] motherhouses." The *Vindicator* indicated the largest communities operating in the diocese were the Ursuline and Humility of Mary Sisters, both of whom recorded ninety-three members at that time.[230]

Hence, in 1990, when Sister Patricia McNicholas assumed her duties as the general superior of the Ursuline Sisters of Youngstown, she understood that her community would need to do more with less. Under these circumstances, she could have been discouraged. Instead, Sister Patricia chose to focus on new opportunities.

During the next six years, she oversaw a major expansion of the motherhouse, the sale of unused acreage to replenish the community's retirement fund and the rise of new and innovative ministries.

Sister Patricia's positive outlook was rooted in her nuanced understanding of the Ursuline Sisters' history, which had involved numerous transformations.

In the 1990s, more than sixty members of the Ursuline community gathered for a group photograph. *Courtesy of the Ursuline Sisters of Youngstown.*

She recognized, for instance, that her first years as an Ursuline Sister reflected a relatively recent stage in the order's development, one characterized by an overarching commitment to teaching.

When Sister Patricia became a professed member of the Ursuline community, her career moved along a path that reflected this ministerial focus. She taught grade school for several years at Saint Charles and Saint Nicholas Schools. After teaching one year at Ursuline High School, she transferred to her alma mater, Cardinal Mooney High School, where she taught between 1971 and 1975.

Shortly after her departure from Cardinal Mooney, however, Sister Patricia made a decision that would eventually take her beyond classroom teaching. In the mid-1970s, she enrolled in summer classes at Cleveland's Saint John's College. She then went on to earn a graduate degree in religious education at The Catholic University of America in Washington, D.C.

Upon her return, Sister Patricia accepted a position at the Diocese of Youngstown's Religious Education Office, where she ultimately assumed the role of director. "We had, at that time, about 16,000 kids, between the public schools and Catholic schools," she explained. "So, it was all about teacher training."

Over the next few years, Sister Patricia secured additional degrees at the University of Notre Dame and United Theological Seminary, a Methodist institution in Dayton, Ohio, where she earned a doctorate in ministry.

Sister Patricia's longstanding interest in ecumenism deepened when she became involved with a group of religious scholars that met regularly in Northeast Ohio and gathered twice a year in Dayton for an "intensive weeklong program."

Significantly, Sister Patricia's years at United Theological Seminary also gave her an opportunity to examine the roots of the Ursuline community, which hinted at a broader mission than she anticipated.

Sister Patricia indicated that her appreciation of Saint Angela's courage and vision was enhanced through conversations she had with a professor at United Theological Seminary, who helped her place the founder's ministry within the context of the tumultuous sixteenth century. "We don't have a lot of Angela's writings, but they're extremely adaptable to the times," Sister Patricia noted.[231]

Sister Patricia's insights into her community's formative years would prepare her for the next phase of her career. As it turned out, her tenure as general superior of the Ursuline community coincided with developments that reflected Saint Angela's recommendation to address the needs of the times.

THE DEVELOPMENT OF URSULINE CENTER

Among the tasks awaiting Sister Patricia and her council in the early 1990s was the need to further upgrade the Ursuline Motherhouse. By that time, efforts to modify the building had become part of an established pattern.

In 1972, just nine years after the facility's completion, Mother Edna Marie Brindle oversaw the conversion of an original novitiate dormitory into bedrooms for retired sisters. Four years later, in 1976, Sister Teresa Winsen supervised the building's insulation and established an archives office in what had been the priests' dining room.

As noted, Sister Mary Conroy, who served as general superior between 1980 and 1984, converted two additional novitiate dormitories into administrative offices and bedrooms, respectively. Later in the decade, of course, Sister Nancy Dawson moved forward on plans to remodel the chapel and dining room while taking steps to improve the sewage system.

Sister Isabel Rudge, who was rounding out the second of two six-year terms as a member of the community's council, recalled that the first major issue on Sister Patricia's agenda was the fate of the motherhouse's swimming pool, which had been donated by contractor Anthony P. O'Horo in 1965 and enclosed in 1966.

By the early 1990s, the pool required expensive repairs, and the community was divided on how to address the situation. At that point, the motherhouse received two unexpected phone calls from corporations expressing an interest in renting the pool for upcoming programs. "So, we decided to fix it," Sister Isabel stated.

This was hardly the only infrastructure issue facing the new superior. Over the years, questions had swirled around the future of Ursuline Preschool and Kindergarten, which was housed in a former private residence on Shields Road across the street from the motherhouse.

Council member Sister Martina Casey, then the principal of Saint Charles School, agreed to temporarily assume leadership of the preschool to evaluate strategies for moving forward. Within a year, she concluded that the aging facility no longer met the needs of the preschool.

The council responded by recommending that the community expand the motherhouse to accommodate new preschool facilities while selling the existing site. "Those were big decisions," Sister Isabel stressed.[232] If this was not enough, the scope of the project soon increased to encompass far more than the creation of a new 11,518-square-foot space for the preschool.

The expanded motherhouse, rechristened as Ursuline Center, would accommodate programs including the Ursuline School of Music, led by Sister Cecilia Morano and Sister Germaine Staron; Speech and Hearing Services, led by Sister LaVerne Weinheimer; the Merici Program for disabled adults; and, eventually, an HIV/AIDS support group, led by Sister Kathleen Minchin, Sister Mary Lee Nalley, Sister Nancy Dawson and Sister Pauline Dalpe.

By the spring of 1993, construction workers were putting finishing touches on the motherhouse's new $2.4 million education wing, which housed six classrooms and a large playroom and rest area, as well as a computer, speech and hearing room. K. Anthony Hayek, the head of the architectural firm of Anthony Hayek Associates, noted that the new education wing would have its own entrance distinct from the motherhouse's main entryway.

Since the new preschool had six classrooms, as opposed to the four it had at the earlier site, the Ursulines predicted that enrollment would rise from 170 to 250.[233]

While Sister Martina served as the preschool's principal, the institution's leadership would gradually reflect a higher level of lay involvement. In the late 1990s, Mary Ann Critell, a former Ursuline nun who had spent fourteen years raising her own family, joined the teaching staff and later assumed the role of director.

Looking back, she recalled that the preschool and kindergarten offered a warm, familial and spiritual atmosphere. "One parent told me that the moment she walked in the door, she felt God's presence," Critell stated. "Over the years, I've been invited to high school graduations, college graduations, weddings, and most recently, baptisms of the children of students I have taught."[234]

As part of the renovation project, the motherhouse's existing adult education center was expanded by 6,735 square feet to accommodate a new auditorium that seated 225 people, an industrial kitchen and two storage rooms. Upon its completion, the center would have its own main entrance and elevator to ensure barrier-free access.

Mary Ann Critell joined the teaching staff of Ursuline Preschool in the 1990s and eventually became the director. *Courtesy of Ursuline Sisters of Youngstown.*

The *Vindicator* reported that the expansion project would be "partially financed by $700,000 through capital improvement funds and the sale of the present kindergarten property."[235]

During the Ursuline Center's dedication on August 29, 1993, the community credited more than a dozen special donors, including the Kilcawley and Christman families, the DeBartolo and York families, the William G. Lyden family, the Rudge and Welsh families, Mr. and Mrs. Daniel O'Horo, the McNicholas Foundation, the Deibel family, attorney John and Dorothy Masternick, the Youngstown Foundation, attorney and Mrs. John M. Newman and the Robert and Maryalyce Herpy family, among others.

Sister Patricia explained in a written statement that over the previous decade, the motherhouse had been the site of "meetings, retreats, support groups, educational activities, speech and hearing services, music lessons [and] Summer Magic day camp." She expressed hope that with the dedication of the Ursuline Center, the community would "be able to increase the number and variety of services available in our own home."[236]

The revamped facility, known as the Ursuline Education and Wellness Center, continues to serve the educational, spiritual and wellness needs of hundreds of people of all ages on a weekly basis, with enrichment classes, spiritual direction and retreats, a labyrinth, a prison ministry, pastoral and bereavement counseling, a prayer shawl ministry, the motherhouse pool ministry, fitness programs for senior citizens and other programs.

Within a year, the community's leaders made another decision that revealed their willingness to address the looming challenges of the future. In 1994, the Ursuline Sisters sold 77 acres of their 138-acre plot in Canfield, thereby raising $900,000 for their ministries while increasing financing for the religious community's retirement fund.

The property was sold to Boardman-based Sorice Construction Inc., which planned a housing development that would "consist of 101 residential lots ranging from one-half acre to three-fourths [of an] acre apiece. The new development was christened the Cloisters in recognition of the fact that the property had been part of the motherhouse's original acreage."

Proceeds from the sale were expected to benefit programs including Beatitude House, a transitional facility for single mothers seeking a better life; the community's HIV/AIDS ministry, which provided a variety of services to area residents; Peace Grows, a program that offered alternatives to violence for local children and adults; and a pastoral services project on the Crow Indian Reservation in Montana, where a sister was then ministering.

Additionally, the funds would help support two center city parochial schools in the Diocese of Youngstown. In an interview, Sister Patricia explained, "With the increase in funding, we may be able to expand our support of many of these programs and also consider new areas of ministry with the poor."[237]

THE STORY OF BEATITUDE HOUSE

The motherhouse's expansion dovetailed with the rise of new ministries that were designed to address the needs of the poor and marginalized. One of these programs was the brainchild of a visionary and energetic nun who was determined to help disadvantaged women and children change their lives.

Sister Margaret "Peggy" Scheetz surprised many of her own peers with the range of skills she brought to the project. Until then, her most visible talents lay in the direction of mathematics and emerging technology. A former teacher at Cardinal Mooney High School, Sister Peggy held advanced degrees in mathematics and computer science.

However, the trajectory of Sister Peggy's life changed in the late 1980s, when she was completing her graduate studies in computer languages at Kent State University. Sister Peggy happened to view a television movie called *God Bless the Child*, an experience she found "truly inspirational."[238]

The 1988 film explores the realities of homelessness from the perspective of a single mother who feels compelled to give up her child for adoption because she no longer believes she can provide for her. The film left an indelible impression on Sister Peggy, and years later, she cited it as an influence on her ministry. "If [the single mother depicted in the film] had just a little bit of support, if she had someone she could've lived with for a month, she would have made it," Sister Peggy explained in a 1994 interview with the *Metro Eye* (now the *Metro Monthly*), a local news publication.[239]

With the film's impact still fresh, Sister Peggy began to volunteer at a site for the homeless maintained by Sisters of the Humility of Mary. When she returned to the Mahoning Valley, she announced her decision to initiate a ministry to benefit the homeless. Sister Nancy Dawson, who was then serving as the community's general superior, offered characteristic encouragement. "Give it a try," she said.[240]

Over the next year, Sister Peggy researched the topic in the Youngstown area and was stunned at the number of local women and children affected by homelessness. She slowly developed the concept of a two-year transitional program for homeless women with children that would help them secure a secondary education and a livable wage.

Launching the project involved the formidable task of securing a house, but Sister Peggy took a sanguine view of the situation. "I made a deal with God that if [He] wanted me to (start the program), He had to find the house," she explained. To improve her odds, she obtained the services of a realtor, "because God needs help."[241] By the early 1990s, the Ursulines' new general superior, Sister Patricia, had become involved, "riding around with her, looking for possible sites."

At one point, the pair learned about John and Dorothy Masternick, local developers of nursing homes and assisted-living campuses who were also known to be philanthropists. The couple agreed to donate a large, Tudor-style home on the city's north side that had served as one of their facilities. Dorothy Masternick christened the new program Beatitude House, a name it has retained ever since.[242]

Confronted with the challenge of turning a former nursing home into a transitional facility for single mothers, Sister Peggy, the daughter of a carpenter, proved she was up to the task. "As the youngest, she used to follow him around," Sister Patricia explained. "So, when she got this empty house, she could do a lot of the smaller work.'"[243] Of course, skills alone weren't enough to realize her vision, and Sister Peggy understood that funding was necessary to move forward.

Beatitude House's earliest support came from the City of Youngstown, which provided $50,000—a substantial sum but not enough to get the organization up and running. "Fortunately, the community was behind the project, and pitched in with services and money," the *Metro Eye* reported. Employees at two local banks helped paint the facility, and carpet and kitchen cabinet retailers agreed "to donate work and materials when Sr. Margaret came to their business with a floor plan of the building." In time, the program benefited from other material donations, including stoves from East Ohio Gas Co. and ceiling fans from Bermann Electric.

Beatitude House opened to the public in the summer of 1991, with Sister Peggy serving as director. The program's first applicants, some of whom were referred by other social service agencies, participated in multiple interviews to determine they were interested in making significant changes in their lives and "not just looking for an inexpensive place to live."

Sister Peggy stressed that all the women involved in the program received a detailed overview of what was expected of them. They were informed that

In 1991, Sister Margaret "Peggy" Scheetz established Beatitude House, a transitional program for homeless single mothers designed to help them become independent. *Courtesy of the Diocese of Youngstown.*

Beatitude House was not merely a home but also "part of a program, and our program demands change, and it's not easy."[244]

Meanwhile, Sister Peggy drew on her quantitative skills to put the organization on a solid economic footing. "She transferred those math skills to accounting, and that chart of accounts was probably in use for the next thirty years," Sister Patricia observed.

Yet the nun also showed a rare ability to connect to the women and children who turned to Beatitude House for assistance. "I still occasionally run into some of the people that were there in the beginning, and they have…nothing but admiration and love for her," Sister Patricia explained.[245]

By the end of the program's first year of operation, Beatitude House had accumulated a surplus of $480,000, which was used to purchase an apartment building across the street from the original structure. By 1994, the nonprofit organization had acquired a second home on Youngstown's north side.[246]

However, in 1997, Beatitude House ran into unexpected difficulties when the organization set out to establish the Potter's Wheel, another transitional facility for homeless women with children that was supposed to operate on Youngstown's west side. A February 1997 *Vindicator* article indicated the proposed facility, based at the former convent at Saint Brendan's Parish, would "house four families on the second floor and would provide vocational training for up to 30 women on the first floor."

Almost immediately, a group of neighborhood residents condemned the program as a violation of the city's zoning laws for residential areas.[247] A spokesman for the group, which called itself the West Side Citizens League, praised the religious community's goals but went on to argue that residents "fear for the safety of their children and feel the project is being rammed down their throats by city officials and the Catholic church."[248]

In the wake of the controversy—which involved angry residents, the Youngstown Zoning Board of Appeals and the Ohio Seventh District Court of Appeals—the future of the Potter's Wheel remained in limbo for the next several years. After a disappointing 1999 ruling against the nonprofit organization by the Seventh District Court of Appeals, a disheartened Sister Peggy framed the outcome as "a sad story about what people think about other people just because they're poor."[249]

The Potter's Wheel survived these legal battles, and variations on the program continue to operate today, but the opposition it faced was an eye-opener for members of the Ursuline religious community. "We spent five years in court," Sister Patricia recalled. "The controversy was clearly motivated by racial bias."[250] In 2001, as the battle over the Potter's Wheel wound down, Sister Peggy Scheetz, who had been diagnosed with terminal brain cancer, became incapacitated and passed away.

Former *Vindicator* columnist Nancy Ward Beeghly, a visible advocate for the Beatitude House program, recalled that Sister Peggy "showed real bravery" in the face of terminal illness. "She continued to work, even when she was on chemotherapy," she recalled.

Beeghly indicated that, as she investigated issues related to poverty, she was shocked to discover that the government showed little interest in helping people become independent from welfare programs. Worse yet, recipients of such aid rarely received much respect. "However, Sister Peggy Scheetz and others in the Beatitude House program treated these women with a high level of respect, which helped them develop self-respect," Beeghly noted.

In the years since Sister Peggy's death, Beatitude House has continued to grow, establishing locations in Mahoning and Ashtabula Counties.

MINISTERING TO PEOPLE WITH HIV/AIDS

The launch of Beatitude House was followed by the establishment in 1993 of the community's HIV/AIDS ministry, spearheaded by a small but energetic group of nuns: Sister Kathleen Minchin, Sister Nancy Dawson, Sister Mary Lee Nalley and Sister Pauline Dalpe. Each sister, in her own way, had become aware of the challenges facing those living with the disease.

Sister Kathleen, who was then serving as a chaplain at a local hospital, knew firsthand that patients with HIV/AIDS were routinely marginalized by physicians and nurses alike. Dismayed, she decided to compare notes with three other nuns who were working together to identify a new ministry. "There were four of us—Sisters Pauline, Nancy, Mary Lee, and me—and we were talking about what Angela would want us to do at this point," Sister Kathleen recalled. "Well, surprisingly, each of us had a story about somebody who had HIV/AIDS."

Sister Kathleen identified a possible starting point for this kind of ministry when another chaplain told her about a local HIV/AIDS support group that had been organized with the help of a Presbyterian minister. Affiliated with Living in the Light, a national HIV/AIDS support program, the group met on Tuesday evenings at a home that was owned by the minister's church near the outskirts of Youngstown's west side.

When Sister Kathleen contacted the group's leader, his response was encouraging. She informed the man that she and three other Ursuline nuns planned to join the next meeting. "We arrived at seven o'clock…and there were about five guys standing near the coffee maker talking," Sister Kathleen explained. After a few more minutes passed, she asked when the group planned to start the meeting.

One of the men looked up with surprise and said, "Yes…we've been waiting for four nuns, but they evidently didn't show up." The sisters instantly realized that the men were unaccustomed to seeing nuns in street clothes, and they introduced themselves.

The meeting opened with a short reading from a handbook supplied by the organization that sponsored the group, but participants soon fell into an uncomfortable silence. "Nobody wanted to say anything," Sister Kathleen observed. "Finally, Nancy Dawson said something like 'hell' or 'damn,' and everyone in the room suddenly exhaled.…So, from that point on, we were accepted."

Within a few weeks, the nuns began to invite speakers to the group to discuss a range of issues related to HIV/AIDS. These speakers included Krista Blake, a young woman from nearby Columbiana County who had contracted AIDS as a teenager during an encounter with a young man. In August 1992, Blake was featured in a *Newsweek* cover story that warned of the relentless spread of the disease, even in rural communities like Columbiana County.

Members of the group were moved by the young woman's hopeful outlook, even as she faced the realities of an incurable disease that would claim her life in 1994 at the age of twenty-two. After Blake's presentation, one member of the group shared his personal fears about dying and lamented the fact that he had received no support from his own faith community. "They all belonged to various churches," Sister Kathleen pointed out. "In the course of that evening, we heard every story in the world about how they were treated by those churches—every church."

In response, the four nuns invited the men to the Ursuline Motherhouse to participate in what they termed a "spiritual support group." For the next two years, the spiritual support group met in one of the facility's conference rooms. As time passed, some of the members' relatives began to show up at meetings to share their feelings and concerns. "You had parents who were afraid to let their son eat off dishes that were in their house," Sister Kathleen recalled. "So, we tried to educate the parents."

Meanwhile, there was an apparent need to educate several members of the Ursuline religious community itself. While most of the sisters welcomed the support group, a small faction questioned the men's presence at the motherhouse. Sister Patricia McNicholas, after learning about the situation, scheduled a community day to discuss popular misconceptions about the disease. "Things got better after that," Sister Kathleen explained.

From there, the ministry developed in ways that few could have anticipated. At the close of one meeting in 1994, Sister Nancy posed a question to the men: "Is there anything else that you need?" After a brief pause, one

The Ursuline Sisters' HIV/AIDS ministry was organized in 1993 by (*left to right*) Sister Kathleen Minchin, Sister Mary Lee Nalley, Sister Nancy Dawson and Sister Pauline Dalpe. The group was honored in a 2018 ceremony marking the ministry's twenty-fifth anniversary. *Courtesy of Ursuline Sisters of Youngstown.*

member of the group explained that most of his peers were dependent on food stamps, which do not cover household items many would treat as necessities, including toilet paper.

Based on the expressed needs of the group, the nuns decided to establish a pantry to help the men secure items they couldn't purchase with food stamps. When the sisters sent a letter requesting support from local churches, they received encouraging responses from several Catholic parishes and a couple of Presbyterian congregations.

To ensure that their pantry operated in an equitable manner, the sisters contacted organizations that maintained similar pantries across the country. These groups advised the sisters to recruit volunteers to staff the pantry while packaging items so that everyone received the same combination of goods. They also suggested that the nuns set a firm schedule for the pantry, and they agreed that it would operate on weekdays from noon to two o'clock in the afternoon.

In June 1994, the community opened Angela's Place, a pantry that provided clients with toiletries and household items while facilitating participation in counseling sessions.[251] On its first day of operation, the pantry, based in a former classroom, drew twenty-five people—a turnout the sisters found encouraging.

At the same time, they faced an unanticipated challenge. "We thought the men would come in, get their bags, and leave," Sister Kathleen explained. "Well, they came in, put their bags down, and continued to sit in the room and talk." Finally, at three o'clock, Sister Kathleen informed the men that they would need to leave because the room was reserved for another program.

A similar scene unfolded at the next giveaway. Sensing a pattern, a proactive volunteer decided to purchase bags of fast food from a nearby Taco Bell restaurant and offered the men a free lunch. It was clear that visitors to Angela's Place wanted more than access to household products; they hungered for a sense of community.

That afternoon, the same volunteer approached Sister Kathleen and suggested the nuns offer a meal shortly after the pantry giveaway. "After all, you have a beautiful auditorium here at the motherhouse," he noted. While Sister Kathleen indicated she was open to the idea, she explained that the community had no dishes that could be used for such a meal. Unfazed, the volunteer indicated that Austintown Fitch High School, located five miles from the motherhouse, had just closed its cafeteria. The school's janitor had saved most of the dishes, and the volunteer had already arranged to purchase them. His subsequent offer to cook the meals paved the way for the motherhouse's Guardian Angel Café.

Open on the third Saturday of every month, the café was designed to provide "a nutritious dinner and a time for socialization for those with HIV/AIDS and their caregivers and companions."[252] In response to the program's growth, Sister Kathleen decided to leave her position as a hospital chaplain to devote herself to the HIV/AIDS ministry.[253]

Like the support group, the café soon attracted some of the men's relatives, which produced another unanticipated challenge. "When the café started, it was just adults," observed Brigid Kennedy, a volunteer for the ministry who currently serves as the chief mission officer for the Ursuline Sisters of Youngstown and the president and CEO of Ursuline Sisters Mission. "As time went on, people began to bring their children."

Kennedy, then a candidate for religious life, understood that the presence of children at the café could be problematic. "You had people in various stages of illness who wanted to talk about adult things, and you had little kids running underfoot," she recalled.

Along with Sister Pauline, Kennedy offered to accompany the children to a nearby conference room and keep them occupied. "That was really the beginning of the children's program," she explained. As she got to know the children, most of whom were from families affected by HIV/AIDS, she learned that many were struggling in school.

Stirred to action, Kennedy volunteered to pick up the children on Tuesday evenings, drive them to the motherhouse and tutor them in various subjects. "We enlisted volunteers to help with the tutoring, and we bought…pizza for the kids," she noted. As the program developed, Kennedy decided that it required a separate building.

Kennedy then approached an uncle who belonged to a group of local businessmen who owned properties throughout Youngstown. One south side property the group owned had recently served as a drug house, but it was then sitting empty. Her uncle offered to donate the house to the program if Kennedy found it suitable.[254] In time, Sister Nancy Dawson, the new general superior, approved the group's decision to reclaim the property, and the formerly dilapidated structure—rechristened Casa Madre—became the locus of a program that offered recreational, social and educational services to children affected by HIV/AIDS.

Kennedy recruited volunteers from her large circle of friends and relatives to refurbish the house. Meanwhile, another volunteer with the HIV/AIDS ministry contacted a friend who owned a car dealership and convinced him to donate a van that could be used to transport the children to and from the facility.

Sister Kathleen then hired a director for the program and scheduled a dedication ceremony. "From there, the program really took off," she recalled. "We had about thirty kids involved. Unfortunately, many of them had HIV/AIDS, and the other kids didn't know about it." Hence, the situation at Casa Madre highlighted yet another challenge facing adults and children dealing with HIV/AIDS: a lack of adequate medical services.

At that point, Sister Kathleen and Kennedy received a phone call from Dr. John S. Venglarcik, an infectious disease specialist based at Youngstown's North Side Hospital. While Dr. Venglarcik had organized a makeshift clinic in a closet located in the hospital's basement, he learned that the hospital's administrators planned to close the facility because it wasn't "remunerative." The physician asked for their help to identify another potential site.

Sister Kathleen and Kennedy contacted Neil Altman, the commissioner of the Youngstown Health Department, which maintained a public clinic that was open several days a week. Altman suggested that Dr. Venglarcik arrange to meet HIV/AIDS patients at the clinic during the hours it was closed to the public. As it turned out, however, many of Altman's colleagues were uncomfortable with this arrangement, which complicated the task of staffing the clinic.

Nevertheless, for five years, the clinic benefited from the services of Dr. Susan Hunt, a physician at the University of Pittsburgh. Her tenure ended unexpectedly, however, when she experienced health problems. Just as the situation at the clinic began to seem hopeless, a local doctor referred the sisters to Dr. Indru P. Limbu, a Nepalese-born infectious disease physician. Dr. Limbu, who was then seeking U.S. citizenship, developed a strong relationship with the Ursuline Sisters.

Years later, when Dr. Limbu was hired as an infectious disease specialist at what is now Mercy Health–St. Elizabeth Youngstown, he resisted his employers' request to end his relationship with the HIV/AIDS clinic. "He told them that he couldn't stop working there because the Ursuline Sisters had been so good to him," Sister Kathleen recalled.

The Ursulines' HIV/AIDS ministry, despite its modest beginnings, filled a hole in medical and social services for area residents living with the disease. Today, the Ursuline Sisters maintain the only clinic in the Mahoning Valley that is dedicated to pediatric and adult HIV testing, HIV healthcare, counseling, case management, patient education, peer support and wrap-around services to adults, adolescents and children living with HIV/AIDS. To date, no infants have been born with HIV/AIDS to mothers under the Ursuline clinic's care.

New Hope Academy

While the Ursulines had diversified their ministries by the 1990s, a relatively small group of nuns remained active at local parish schools. One of them was Sister Mary Dunn, whose career reflected her commitment to educational outreach in center city neighborhoods.

During a 1991 interview with the *Vindicator*, Sister Mary, then the principal of Saint Patrick School, highlighted the significant role parochial schools continued to play in low-income neighborhoods.

When asked about a recent countywide fundraising campaign that raised $115,000 to support two center-city institutions, including Saint Patrick and Immaculate Conception Schools, Sister Mary responded by describing the wide range of services her school provided to families in the neighborhood.

She pointed out that students "who are hungry can't learn unless they're fed and clothed and helped to get well."[255]

As the decade progressed, however, the future of urban parochial schools like Saint Patrick became more uncertain. In January 1992, the diocese announced, once again, that special collections would be taken up at local churches to support Youngstown's two "financially strapped" parish schools. Bishop James Malone issued a letter to churches in Mahoning County, which stated, "We have a mission to bring the good news and gospel values to everyone, especially to the poorer members of the community."[256]

This time, the campaign goal was $125,000, and advocates of the schools reached out to private donors, parochial school students and urban Protestant churches. Despite these efforts, however, the campaign fell short of its goal by a substantial $60,000. In response, diocesan school superintendent Dr. Nicholas Wolsonovich issued an appeal for broader support.

While the diocese was able to keep the schools open through contributions from anonymous donors, more questions arose about the community's willingness to support center-city schools like Immaculate Conception and Saint Patrick.[257]

To make matters worse, the scope of diocesan fundraising campaigns had widened as more local urban parochial schools experienced financial difficulty. In early 1995, the diocese launched an eighteen-month, $451,000 fundraising campaign designed to create "long-term financial stability" to five struggling parish schools: Immaculate Conception, Saint Patrick, Saint Anthony, Saint Edward and Saint Dominic.[258]

The next month, the diocese announced that the fundraising campaign had fallen short of its goal of $451,000, raising a total of just $100,000. Shortly thereafter, the diocese's efforts to attract an additional $150,000 from seventy individual donors also proved disappointing.[259] This combination of events contributed to the closure of Saint Patrick School at the end of the 1995–96 academic year.

In what would become a common practice, the school building was put to a similar use shortly after Saint Patrick's closure. In 1996, the former parish school became the site of New Hope Academy, a "Christ-centered school" that was jointly established by the Ursuline Sisters of Youngstown, the Catholic Diocese of Youngstown and the Northeastern Ohio Synod of the Evangelical Lutheran Church of America.

A driving force at the new school was Sister Elizabeth "Betty" Schuster, who had served most recently as an administrative assistant at Holy Family School in neighboring Poland. A native of Rockville Centre, New

Sister Elizabeth "Betty" Schuster assists students at New Hope Academy, an ecumenical institution located at the former site of Youngstown's Saint Patrick School. *Courtesy of Ursuline Sisters of Youngstown.*

York, Sister Betty was introduced to the Ursuline Sisters of Youngstown in 1992, when she became involved in Ursuline Companions in Mission, a national program that encouraged the involvement of lay people in the order's ministries.

Sister Betty volunteered as a layperson for two years at Beatitude House before entering the Ursuline Sisters in 1994. A former health and physical education instructor with a graduate degree in health science, Sister Betty was well prepared to serve as a teacher at New Hope Academy. During the academy's 1998–99 school year, she was appointed assistant principal.[260]

For Sister Isabel Rudge, a member of the school's board of directors, New Hope Academy's ecumenical message resonated. Raised in a family of mixed English and Irish ancestry, Sister Isabel grew up with the knowledge that some of her relatives belonged to the Episcopal Church, which informed her approach to denominational differences.

Therefore, Sister Isabel was deeply disappointed when New Hope Academy faltered amid growing competition from urban charter schools. "I was on the board when we were closing that school…and it was very sad," she said.[261]

During its brief five-year run, however, New Hope Academy deepened the goodwill that characterized the relationship between Saint Patrick Parish and residents of the surrounding neighborhood. Today, the former parish school building serves as the site of a charter school managed by Summit Academy Inc., an enterprise that operates three charter schools in Youngstown—all of which are housed in former parochial school buildings.

A PILGRIMAGE TO BRESCIA

In 1996, the same year New Hope Academy opened its doors, the Ursuline Sisters selected a special venue for their annual retreat, a period traditionally set aside for reflection and prayer "in order to be renewed for ministry."

In July that year, under the leadership of Sister Patricia McNicholas, forty-six members of the religious community participated in a pilgrimage to Italy, where they visited sites connected to the life and ministry of Saint Angela Merici, who organized the Company of Saint Ursula in 1535.

Their itinerary opened with a visit to the northern Italian city of Brescia, where Angela had lived and worked in the years leading up to the community's establishment. During their visit to Brescia, the sisters resided at Casa Saint Angela, a retreat house located near the humble edifice where Angela spent her final years.

Their other destinations in Northern Italy included Desenzano, Angela's birthplace, and Assisi, the hometown of Saint Francis of Assisi, to whom Saint Angela was devoted. The retreat concluded with a visit to the Italian capital of Rome, where the sisters toured Saint Peter's Basilica, the Sistine Chapel and other historical sites.

Sister Marlene LoGrasso called attention to the spiritual nature of the journey. "We were pilgrims, not tourists," she explained. "Over the years, many of us had read about the life of St. Angela, so it was a powerful experience to visit the places where she lived and worked. We were literally walking in her footsteps."[262]

Similarly, Sister Diane Toth, another participant in the pilgrimage, indicated that she felt the saint's presence during a visit to the Church of Sant'Afra, where Saint Angela attended mass. The nun was "astounded" when she viewed the preserved remains of the saint, which are displayed in the church. "Angela was such a tiny woman, with little in the way of education, but her impact was incredible," she said.[263]

Dozens of Ursuline Sisters participated in a 1996 pilgrimage to Italy, where they visited sites connected to the life of Saint Angela Merici. *Courtesy of Ursuline Sisters of Youngstown.*

Each participant in the retreat was struck by the radically different environment they encountered upon their arrival in Rome. "There had been relatively few tourists in places like Brescia," Sister Marlene noted. "When we visited the Sistine Chapel, however, we were packed in like sardines. It was extremely hot...and over the noise of the crowd, you could hear the tour guides screaming, 'Silencio! Silencio!'"

She also took note of the fact that images of Saint Angela throughout Rome presented her in the habit of a French Ursuline. "We know that Angela advised members of her company to dress in the manner of the times," she said. "That's the way she's depicted in the paintings and statues we saw in Brescia and Desenzano, but not in Rome."[264]

For one member of the group, however, the journey to the Italian capital was "a dream come true." Sister Diane, a student of Italian art, was delighted to experience firsthand the architectural and artistic masterpieces that, until then, she had only read about.[265]

Ministering to Marginalized Groups in North America

Although the Ursuline Sisters of Youngstown had a long track record of formal education, individual members of the community had been involved in missionary work as early as the 1890s, when Mother Lawrence McCaffrey, at the request of her counterpart in Toledo, sent two local nuns to work at Montana's Saint Labre Indian School, where they remained from 1893 to 1897.

More than seventy years later, in 1969, two local Ursuline nuns, Sister Mary Ann Diersing and Sister Petra Chavez, were sent to Peru, where they worked with the Ursuline Sisters of the Roman Union, who ran two schools in the Peruvian capital of Lima. They came back to the United States in 1972, only to return to Peru four years later to continue their missionary work. Sister Mary Ann, who worked as a pastoral minister at a mission along the Amazon River, recalled "traveling to all the villages by boat, training the lay leaders in each village, and teaching religion to the children."[266]

In the 1990s, Sister Dorothy Kundracik and Sister Norma Raupple continued this tradition with their outreach to marginalized groups in North America. Sister Dorothy's ministry at Montana's Crow Reservation and Sister Norma's work with Spanish-speaking residents of Brownsville, Texas, and Matamoros, Mexico, underscored the fact that the Ursuline community had moved beyond classroom education to address the needs of diverse populations.

In the spring of 1990, Sister Dorothy Kundracik was teaching third-grade students at Saint Joan of Arc School in Canton, Ohio, when she became enthralled with a way of life she had never experienced. "I was teaching Native American culture to my students, so I was reading and absorbing everything," she recalled. "At the time, we were sending money to Labre Mission in Montana....I said, 'I want to go there.'"

Sister Dorothy eventually contacted Father Charles Robinson, Order of Friars Minor Capuchin (OFM Cap.), the pastor of Saint Dennis Parish on the Crow Reservation. When she expressed an interest in volunteering, the priest didn't mince his words: "You want to come? When can you come? How long can you stay? And where do I pick you up?"

On July 2, 1990, Sister Dorothy boarded a plane for Montana to volunteer for six weeks of ministry at the Crow Reservation. Upon her arrival, she was overwhelmed by the area's dramatic landscape and arid climate. "The reservation is in the eastern part of Montana, so it's more like the Badlands of the Dakotas," she noted. "The summer temperature was 90 degrees in the daytime, with no humidity."

If Sister Dorothy fell in love with the region's climate and scenery, she was equally charmed by the people she encountered. When she attended her first wedding on the reservation, she was struck by the community's casual approach to time. "It's not two o'clock or three o'clock; it's when we're ready," Sister Dorothy explained. "I was comfortable with that because I always had trouble with punctuality."[267]

By the end of Sister Dorothy's six-week ministry, Father Robinson informed the Ursuline nun she was welcome to stay longer, "as the people appreciated her manner and efforts." At that point, though, Sister Dorothy had a professional commitment to resume her work at Saint Joan of Arc School, where she taught for another year.

In 1992, she applied to teach sixth-grade students at Saint Labre Indian School in Ashland, Montana, and returned to the Crow Reservation, where she became the director of religious education at Saint Dennis Parish.[268]

During the first three years of her stay in Montana, Sister Dorothy taught evening classes to residents who were preparing to take the GED (general educational development) test. Meanwhile, her flexible daytime schedule

Sister Dorothy Kundracik (*right*) bonds with members of the Crow Nation while engaged in missionary work at the Crow Reservation in Montana. *Courtesy of Ursuline Sisters of Youngstown.*

enabled her to attend classes dealing with bicultural society at Little Big Horn College, where she tutored students in algebra and offered informal training in campus ministry.

Aware of the prevalence of chemical dependence on the reservation, Sister Dorothy participated in programs for recovering addicts, which were described as pilgrimages. "I was involved in about thirty weekend pilgrimages during my five years in Montana," she recalled. "It's a twelve-step program, and as part of the fifth step, you're supposed to share your experiences with someone and explain the ways in which you need help."

While most of the reservation's recovering addicts elected to speak to a priest, Sister Dorothy quickly gained the trust of those with whom she interacted. "I felt as though I were hearing confessions because they were so trusting and got so personal," she explained. "They learned that I didn't repeat anything that they told me."[269]

Aware of the dual nature of the spirituality practiced by the Crow tribe, Sister Dorothy seized on opportunities to participate in both Catholic and Native rituals while also studying Crow music, ritual dancing and art. She was invited to clan hand games, or guessing competitions that involve two pairs of bones, and vibrant college pow wows.

Sister Dorothy felt especially privileged to visit members of the tribe during such sacred events as the Sundance, an ancient renewal ceremony held at the time of the summer solstice.[270] She acknowledged that she did not participate in the ceremony itself, which involves an arduous three-day fast. Father Robinson advised her, however, that she could bring dampened cattail reeds and peppermint to ease the discomfort of participants who had refrained from drinking water for a couple of days.

Sister Dorothy experienced a wide range of emotions during one sacred ritual in which the prayer leader blessed her by tapping her repeatedly with a large eagle feather. The leader asked her to focus silently on a prayer request, and Sister Dorothy quietly begged forgiveness for the atrocities that European Americans had inflicted on Natives. "No words passed between us, but I was overcome by a feeling of forgiveness that went beyond anything I had experienced during the Sacrament of Confession," she said.

Ultimately, she was left with the impression that mainstream Americans had much to gain from Native culture. "The Crow people have a whole spirituality that is centered around respect for the earth, respect for nature and people—things we desperately need," Sister Dorothy observed.[271]

Before her departure from Montana in June 1996, Sister Dorothy was adopted by a Native woman known as Evelyn Old Elk, while a Native man,

Arlie Stops, presented her with a Crow name, Bah ii wi she iche, which means "good teacher of many children."[272] "I experienced far more culture shock coming home to Ohio," she recalled. "I loved my work in Montana."[273]

Like Sister Dorothy, Sister Norma Raupple showed a strong interest in other cultures, as well as an openness to new challenges. She recalled that she enjoyed her work as a director of religious education at suburban parishes like Saint Vincent de Paul Parish (Vienna) and Saint Jude Parish (Columbiana). At the same time, she looked forward to taking on a similar position at Youngstown's Immaculate Conception Parish. "I went to Immaculate in 1988 because Father Phil Conley had a vision of welcoming Black Catholics," she explained.

Sister Norma described her ten years at Immaculate Conception as "transformative," given that her previous ministries focused on homogeneous populations. "I valued working with people in the neighborhood and interacting with African American families," she recalled. "Learning to be with other cultures was enriching."

During the late 1990s, Sister Norma became engaged in a dialogue with Ursuline communities throughout North America. She noted that the Ursuline Sisters of Youngstown are affiliated with a loose federation of Ursuline nuns living in the United States, Canada and Mexico. "Some of us got the idea that we should develop a program to immerse ourselves in Hispanic cultures, since so many Hispanic people are Catholic," she recalled. "This would ensure that we would be more comfortable with—and enriched by—those cultures in the future."

When she presented a proposal to the North American group, they accepted it, and five sisters applied to participate in the program. The next step involved selecting a destination: "We wanted to identify the poorest place we could go and live with the people." A likely destination was Brownsville, Texas, an impoverished community situated on the United States–Mexico border.

In September 1997, the five nuns who had volunteered for the program arrived at the border town with little more than the clothes on their backs. "We wanted to be poor missionaries," Sister Norma observed. "We wanted to start out without a house or a car or a job…to see how we would respond." Early on, the group benefited from the assistance of a Dominican nun who located a house in Brownsville that was available to rent. The same sister eventually identified a used car that was for sale. In the interim, however, the nuns relied on the community's bus service, carrying their meager belongings in Styrofoam bedrolls.

Sister Norma's main obstacle in Brownsville was the language difference. Although the community is located within the borders of the United States, few people there communicated in English. "It was a border town, so it felt very much like Mexico," she explained. "It was challenging because the other four nuns were fluent in Spanish, and they could interact with people."

Sister Norma's lack of fluency surprised her, given that she had prepared for her ministry by studying Spanish at Youngstown State University, where she received excellent grades. The next summer, she attempted to remedy this problem by spending three weeks taking classes at a language school near Cuernavaca, Mexico. In the end, though, Sister Norma derived more benefits from her interactions with the Mexican sisters living in Brownsville, Texas, and neighboring Matamoros, Mexico.[274]

As Sister Norma became more comfortable with the Spanish language, she began to teach English to Mexican American adults while working as a teacher's aide for a bilingual reading program at Brownsville's Palm Grove Elementary School. In time, Sister Norma's group opened an all-purpose room at the school that housed computers and an English-language library featuring books provided by Youngstown-area donors.

In the period leading up to the 1998–99 school year, Sister Norma was hired as an instructor for adult learners.[275]

Not surprisingly, Sister Norma's integration into the community heightened her awareness of local challenges. "We found out that the primary needs were education and health care," she explained. "As a nonprofit, we could write grants that helped us address some of those needs." When it became clear healthcare was practically nonexistent in the Mexican community of Matamoros, which was located across the border, the group helped organize a clinic there.

The facility's location reflected the area's extreme poverty, given that it sat on a garbage dump that had become the site of a makeshift village for the homeless. "We knew there were plenty of respiratory issues, a lot of skin problems," Sister Norma observed. "The people there were just living in shacks made out of pallets and garbage bags."

The group befriended a Mexican woman who was a trained physician, and she soon became a partner in their ministry. In time, the physician became one of fifteen local women who embraced the mission of the Ursulines and gathered informally as associates of the order.

While the Ursuline Sisters involved in ministry at the United States–Mexico border recognized the value of their practical contributions, they also

Sister Norma Raupple (*back row, third from left*) is shown with young adult volunteers and participants in an outreach program aimed at immigrant families. *Courtesy of Ursuline Sisters of Youngstown.*

understood the importance of showing solidarity with the people "by living simply, sharing our resources and striving to be an empowering presence."

Since her return to the Mahoning Valley in 2007, Sister Norma's ministries have included outreach programs for immigrant families, which were initially facilitated by Beatitude House.

She noted that her earlier involvement in the program at Brownsville and Matamoros underscored the fact that her religious community had taken a broader view of what ministry could entail. "If you want to talk about how the Ursuline Sisters have expanded their mission, a good example would be that my community supported me when I went to the Texas-Mexico border for ten years," Sister Norma observed.[276]

The Ursuline Sisters' flexibility would become more apparent as the community moved into the twenty-first century.

8

"THE FUTURE IS BRIGHT"

O n the afternoon of June 7, 2006, Sister Charlotte Italiano was visibly moved as she watched twelve eighth-grade students participate in the final graduation ceremony of Immaculate Conception School. "This is bittersweet," she said. "We are very, very sad."[277]

The ceremony marked the imminent closure of an educational institution that had prevailed for more than 120 years. Immaculate Conception's brick schoolhouse, completed in 1905, had towered above the surrounding neighborhood for more than a century as it was transformed by forces that included urban renewal, highway construction, depopulation and deindustrialization.

Significantly, Sister Charlotte herself was a product of the parish school. In an institution staffed by Ursuline nuns, she found a dedicated mentor in Sister Anne Lynch, who planted the seeds of a religious vocation. When she graduated from Immaculate Conception School, Sister Charlotte, along with her twin sister, Rose, attended Ursuline High School, then owned and operated by the Ursuline Sisters.

In 1950, she enrolled at Youngstown College, where she balanced her coursework with teaching responsibilities at three elementary schools. Sister Charlotte entered the novitiate in 1955, after earning a bachelor's degree in education. "So, I was about twenty-three when I entered—a bit older than most of the other novices," she noted.[278]

During her long career, Sister Charlotte would serve as a teacher, administrator or consultant at eight Catholic schools: Saint Ann (Youngstown),

In the late 1950s, the staff of Immaculate Conception School was dominated by Ursuline Sisters, whose long association with that institution ended with the school's closure in 2006. *Courtesy of Saint Angela Merici Parish.*

Saint Charles (Boardman), Saint Rose (Girard), Immaculate Conception, Holy Family (Poland), Saint Patrick (Youngstown), Saint Joseph the Provider (Campbell) and Ursuline Preschool and Kindergarten (Canfield). Her tenure as principal of Holy Family School lasted twenty-six years.

Yet Sister Charlotte's expertise as an administrator could not ensure the survival of Immaculate Conception School, which faced crippling challenges by the time she became principal in the fall of 2005. After decades of news reports predicting the parish school's demise, even the institution's strongest supporters were prepared for its eventual closure.

An article marking the event indicated that Immaculate Conception's enrollment, which approached seven hundred in the 1960s, had fallen to a record low of sixty-three during the 2005–06 academic year.

Sister Charlotte acknowledged that the institution's fate was scarcely an isolated incident. On the morning Sister Charlotte announced that her school would suspend operations, another local Catholic institution held its final graduation ceremony. The *Vindicator* reported that the southside parish school of Saint Matthias, which had served a mostly Slovak American neighborhood since 1917, would not reopen for the 2006–07 academic year.[279]

Media reports on the two school closings undoubtedly saddened those Youngstown area residents who viewed parochial schools as a permanent (and desirable) fixture of the urban landscape.

During its years of operation, however, Immaculate Conception School exemplified the Ursuline Sisters' commitment to the city's poorest families, and its legacy can be discerned in the contributions of those whose lives were enhanced by its presence in a declining neighborhood.

Shelia Triplett, the CEO of Mahoning-Youngstown Community Action Partnership, is one of almost one hundred Ursuline associates. *Courtesy of Ursuline Sisters of Youngstown.*

The school's alumni have included such leaders as Shelia (Jackson) Triplett, who currently serves as the CEO of Mahoning-Youngstown Community Action Partnership (MYCAP), a nonprofit designed to mobilize and utilize resources to increase the quality of life for low-income residents throughout the area. Triplett brings to her position a personal awareness of the challenges arising from poverty, as she was born on Youngstown's east side to a young single parent.

Triplett's involvement with Immaculate Conception Church began when an associate pastor, Father Ralph J. Friedrich, reached out to her family. Her subsequent enrollment at the parish school as a third-grade student paved the way for her enduring relationship with the Ursuline Sisters. As a young adult, she was drawn to a career in social work. "Part of this impulse was nurtured through my experiences at Immaculate…with the whole nature of Catholic education, which encouraged you to take care of people less fortunate than you," she noted.

Triplett reconnected with the Ursuline Sisters in the early 1990s, when she enrolled her son in Immaculate Conception School. There, he bonded with Sister Elizabeth "Betty" Schuster, who taught at the school. "Sr. Betty loved my son, who was always getting into a little bit of trouble," she explained. "When the other teachers were about to pull their hair out, they would call Sr. Betty…and she could get him to do the right thing."

At some point, Sister Betty informed Triplett about a program for homeless single mothers that was then being developed by her good friend Sister Margaret "Peggy" Scheetz. "I was privy to conversations between them when Sr. Peggy began laying the foundations for what became Beatitude House," she recalled. "I knew the program was going to involve work with homeless women and that it would focus on education." Intrigued by the concept, Triplett agreed to serve on the nonprofit's first board.

Later, at the request of Sister Betty, Triplett became the organization's transitional housing director, a position she held for several years before returning to MYCAP.

Today, Triplett serves on the Ursuline Sisters Mission board, which oversees various ministries, including Beatitude House. "Many of those women who found themselves in a safe and secure environment just blossomed," she noted. "In the absence of that program, I don't think they would have had that chance."

Triplett stressed that her view of the Ursuline Sisters has evolved over time. "As a child, I thought about the Ursulines in their capacity as teachers," Triplett acknowledged. "When I look at them now, I see them as leaders in the community, advocating for the poor and disadvantaged, in whatever way that needs to manifest itself."[280]

In 2006, Triplett became an Ursuline associate, a layperson who participates in the order's prayer life while sharing time and expertise to support its ministries. She is one of almost one hundred Ursuline associates who are working together to bring the Sisters' mission into the future, even as the religious community itself continues to decline in numbers. The program's vitality is a testament to the network of relationships the Ursulines have developed through schools, parishes, nonprofit organizations and other forms of community outreach.

ORIGINS OF THE URSULINE ASSOCIATES PROGRAM

Introduced in 2001, the Ursuline associates program came out of earlier efforts to develop a network of women interested in deepening their spirituality. The Company of Angela, established in 1977, began selecting members in 1981 under the leadership of Sister Nancy Dawson and Sister Jacqueline Herpy.

Designed to present members of the Ursuline religious community "as contemporary women in the Church," the organization extended invitations to "women, married, single, divorced, who wish to deepen their personal prayer, pray with others, share faith through dialogue and respond to the call of discipleship and service."

By the early 1990s, the group claimed eighty-two members around the diocese.[281] The Company of Angela proved to be an early stage in the development of what became a vibrant Ursuline associates program—involving women and men—that supports the community and its ministries.

In September 2001, a memo announcing the introduction of an associates program included a modern American translation of one of Saint Angela Merici's famous exhortations to members of her community: "Do something, get moving, be confident, risk new things, stick with it, get on your knees, then be ready for Big Surprises!" This rousing statement was supplemented by references to post–Vatican II theology, which stressed "the universality of the call to active ministry and communal spirituality."

The memo explained that in response to new models of "lay-religious collaboration" in the church, the Ursulines planned to "provide an opportunity for women and men to become associated with the community in a manner other than vowed membership." A six- to nine-month orientation process, later called a formation period, involved the study and discussion of the life and ministry of Saint Angela, an overview of the history and charism of the Ursuline Sisters of Youngstown and discussions on spirituality, prayer and community. This was followed by a retreat, a period of prayer and reflection.

Once associates had formalized their commitment through prayer and ritual, a commitment statement was signed by the general superior, the director of the program and the new associate. All associates received a medal of Saint Angela Merici and were given an opportunity to renew their commitment on an annual basis.[282]

Notably, most members of the first class were former Ursuline Sisters. They included Mary Yvo Assion, who had spent eight years in the community before moving on to a career as a public school teacher, getting married and raising a family.

Assion explained that her decision to leave the order followed a long period of prayer and reflection. She recalled that her first teaching assignment as an Ursuline Sister was at Saint Rose School in Girard. "I was so excited about getting my own classroom and being independent," she said. "But when it came time for me to take another set of vows, I questioned myself: 'Is this what God really wants me to do?'"

After leaving the Ursuline community, Assion taught religious education at a local parish and eventually returned to college to obtain more credentials. She later became an instructor in the Boardman Township School District.

Assion became aware of the Ursuline associates program during a phone conversation with Sister Therese Ann Rich, who noted that each member of the community was asked to provide the name of someone who might wish to participate. "It was up to us to determine how we could best support the sisters and their mission," Assion explained.

As an educator with a graduate degree in early childhood education, Assion decided to focus on Ursuline Preschool. Working with Ruthanne Grant and Mary Ann Critell, both Ursuline associates and former nuns, Assion introduced a program for two-year-olds and their parents or guardians that encouraged creative interaction. "We taught songs and did little art projects," she said. "We had mothers, nannies, grandmothers, and fathers who came in to participate…and they saw how important it was to move in this direction." Since then, Assion has provided volunteer support for many programs, including Beatitude House and the HIV/AIDS ministry.[283]

While the Ursuline associates program was initially dominated by women, more men have become involved. Among them is Ray Novotny, who has volunteered his expertise to the community since 2002, when he retired from his job as a sales manager at a local business. "I was doing a little bit of volunteer work here and there," Novotny recalled. "Then Sister Nancy Dawson said, 'Get your tail over here and help us out at the Ursuline Center.'"

In 2001, Sister Nancy Dawson met with a few of the community's legal and financial advisors, including Elaine Parella, Michael Holliday and attorneys Frank Mastriana and John Newman. *Courtesy of Ursuline Sisters of Youngstown.*

As the director of the center, Sister Nancy asked Novotny to serve a six-year term as president of its board. Three years into his tenure as board president, Novotny became an Ursuline associate. After discovering that the Ursulines had lost substantial revenue when an organization withdrew its programming, he advised them to conduct an asset evaluation. "We knew the motherhouse had a pool," Novotny stated. "But almost nothing was going on there, apart from a small program with a local assisted-care facility."

Drawing on his years of marketing experience, Novotny guided the Ursulines as they increased the pool's usage from hosting fifty people a week to about three hundred people a week. With the support of associates like Novotny, the Ursulines have introduced aquatics classes and turned a meeting room into a part-time venue for an exercise program directed at senior citizens. The community also rented space to North Canton–based Walsh University, which maintained a campus at the motherhouse for more than a decade.[284]

During this period, Ray's wife, Eileen Walsh Novotny, who eventually earned a certificate in spiritual direction at Cleveland's John Carroll University, served as a part-time program director at the Ursuline Center.

In 2008, as the center's program director, Eileen Novotny launched a prayer shawl ministry that focused initially on participants in the community's HIV/AIDS ministry. Over the years, volunteers for the ministry, who live throughout the diocese, have produced more than four thousand shawls, some of which have been distributed to local hospitals and hospice centers.

More recently, Novotny's volunteers have knitted protective socks for Water for Blessings, a ministry of the Ursuline Sisters of Louisville, Kentucky, designed to train families in the use of Sawyer Point One filters to create potable water after hurricanes and other disasters. "The socks enable the sisters to safely deliver the filters to the families who need them," Novotny explained.[285]

Novotny and other Ursuline associates have engaged friends and acquaintances who eventually joined the program. Ursuline associate Peggy Eicher, for instance, was encouraged to volunteer at the motherhouse by Eileen Novotny's husband, Ray. As Ray Novotny prepared to leave his position as president of the center's board, he suggested that Eicher join the body.

Around that time, Sister Mary Ann Coz, who was then in charge of the motherhouse grounds, proposed a campus walk-through that would have a fundraising component. The event was intended, in part, to showcase the motherhouse's new labyrinth, which had been designed and donated by local businessman Jack Donadee.[286]

Sister Nancy, who was serving her third term as superior, enlisted Eicher's assistance to prepare the motherhouse grounds for the event.[287] Eicher received moral support from her husband, Dan, a convert to Catholicism. "I never dreamed that I would become an Ursuline Associate," he admitted. "But I liked what they were doing, and I got involved in that way."[288]

To prepare the grounds, Peggy Eicher enlisted the help of young volunteers associated with faith-sharing groups at her parish. These groups included teenagers whom the Eichers had mentored over the years, and they agreed to spread mulch and complete other landscaping tasks on the motherhouse grounds.

Impressed with the results, Sister Nancy asked Peggy Eicher to play a more consistent role in grounds maintenance as the motherhouse's director of operations. In response, Eicher contacted the Mahoning County Sheriff's Office to inquire about the availability of day reporters, or non-felons who engage in community service. "Sometimes we had six people, and sometimes we had twenty-six people," Eicher noted. "We would start in the spring and go through October.…All sorts of things were accomplished."[289]

Sister Nancy noted that since the program's inception, Ursuline associates have become involved in practically every aspect of the religious community's ministries and operations. "Some people have realized, through prayer and discernment, that you can do a lot of wonderful things by being associated with spirituality, but without necessarily living that structured religious life," she added. "I think feeding on that spirituality has been a real gift of God—for all of us."

Dorothy Day House of Hospitality

Since November 2009, dozens of Ursuline associates have taken advantage of opportunities to volunteer at Dorothy Day House of Hospitality, a haven for the disadvantaged that was established in partnership with the Sisters of the Humility of Mary, based in neighboring Villa Maria, Pennsylvania, and lay members of Youngstown Catholic Worker.

Situated in a former funeral home on a neglected stretch of Youngstown's Belmont Avenue, the facility is one of more than 180 Catholic Worker houses operating worldwide. Its policies are modeled on the principles of journalist and social activist Dorothy Day, who cofounded the Catholic Worker Movement with Peter Maurin in 1933.

Throughout her career, Day was a passionate advocate for "non-violence in the pursuit of justice and hospitality for the impoverished." Sister Ann McManamon, Humility of Mary (HM), the house's longtime director, reflected Day's dedication to the poor, residing on the premises until her retirement.

The impact of the program was evident within a few years of its establishment. According to a July 2013 article in the *Vindicator*, Dorothy Day House had served forty-eight thousand meals and provided three thousand showers to visitors since opening its doors a few years earlier.

Dinners served at the house are provided by donors, including the Ursuline and Humility of Mary Associates, Mercy Health–Saint Elizabeth Youngstown Hospital, Villa Maria Education and Spirituality Center, local restaurants, medical professionals, civic organizations and individual laypeople.[290]

Associate Linda McClure explained that Dorothy Day House, unlike the more institutional programs of its kind, features a "home-like" environment in which visitors are treated as guests. "The house only holds so many people, and some guests are asked to relax in a waiting area until there's room at the table," McClure added. "So, you have an opportunity to interact with people."[291]

Linda McClure volunteers with her husband, Larry (also an Ursuline associate), who prepares meals at Dorothy Day House and often serves them. He explained that various individuals and organizations donate portions of the meals served at the house, with some preparing the main course, while others provide side dishes and desserts.

When a local caterer who supplied a large percentage of main courses announced her retirement, McClure met with fellow members of the Knights of Columbus, a religious fraternal organization, and asked them to step in. Since then, McClure has made similar arrangements with Saint Luke's Parish and the Saint Vincent de Paul Society.

As a volunteer for several organizations focused on the needs of the poor, McClure insisted that Dorothy Day House is different. "At Dorothy Day House, you have a chance to get to know people," he explained. "You're not just feeding them physically, but you're also feeding their souls."[292]

Since Sister Ann's retirement in April 2023, Dorothy Day House of Hospitality has been led by a two-member coordinating team that comprises Ursuline associate Dan Wakefield and Valeria Gonvalves. Wakefield

Sister Norma Raupple (*fourth from left*) oversees volunteers at Dorothy Day House of Hospitality, a ministry founded in a 2009 partnership with the Sisters of the Humility of Mary. Also pictured are Colleen Flanagan, Paulette Smith, Flora Schneider, Patty Canton, Micki Biasella, Mickey Fata and Ray Novotny. *Courtesy of Ursuline Sisters of Youngstown.*

noted that the program relies on volunteers. "Nobody receives a salary or compensation for the work that is done," he said.

The program's organizational structure is also unique, Wakefield added. Apart from the coordinating team, Dorothy Day House is managed by a core team that "meets on a monthly basis to discuss successes, concerns, and ideas."

As Wakefield assumed a leadership role at Dorothy Day House, he reflected on Sister Ann's extraordinary dedication. "For over thirteen years, she worked to create a space that was true to the mission and vision of Dorothy Day and the Catholic Worker Movement," he stated. "She was instrumental in getting volunteers and donations to keep the house going, and to educate volunteers and the larger Youngstown community about care for the poor."[293]

Today, in addition to providing dinners and showers, Dorothy Day House has become a venue for monthly roundtable discussions on issues ranging from the plight of refugees to the plague of human trafficking.

RECONFIGURING THE MOTHERHOUSE

In 2011, two years after the establishment of Dorothy Day House of Hospitality, the Ursuline Sisters embarked on yet another major reconfiguration of their motherhouse. The three-phase project was not only designed to improve conditions for the sisters living at the motherhouse but also to increase the facility's value as a community resource.

Working in collaboration with Paul Ricciuti and Youngstown-based BSHM Architects, Sister Nancy Dawson, as general superior, developed a master plan for the motherhouse that identified the most efficient use of space that had not been fully utilized.

Phase I of the project involved creating twenty-four barrier-free apartments on two floors comprising about 23,000 square feet of space for sisters living in the east wing of the motherhouse. "We wanted to get away from the concept of individual bedroom areas, which were really like cells, very monastic, with bathrooms in the center of the building," Ricciuti recalled. "Those rooms were about 10 feet wide, so we took three of them and created a bedroom area, a bathroom area, and a living room area. This project was essentially to make the space more livable for a shrinking population."[294]

During this phase of the project, estimated to cost $1.7 million, the facility's living spaces were renovated according to universal design principles. The renovations included the introduction of private bathrooms with handicapped accessibility, while "heating and ventilation systems were installed to bring the building's infrastructure into the 21st century," a community newsletter reported.

This phase of the project was partly funded through a $25,000 grant from the Springfield, Maryland–based nonprofit SOAR (Support Our Aging Religious).[295]

Phases II and III, carried out over the next two years, involved the relocation of the community's administrative offices and the construction of eleven one-bedroom apartments and one two-bedroom apartment in the western wing of the motherhouse. As part of Phase II, the James and Coralie Centofanti Foundation provided the Ursulines with a technology grant of $20,000 to establish a ministry conference room, which cost about $400,000.

Phase III—the most groundbreaking aspect of the reconfiguration project—involved the establishment of Ursuline Sisters Senior Living, a new apartment ministry designed to provide housing for moderate-income senior citizens in the Mahoning Valley.

The Ursuline Motherhouse currently serves as a major resource for the Mahoning Valley. *Courtesy of Ursuline Sisters of Youngstown.*

Estimated to cost about $1.2 million, this phase benefited from the generosity of private donors, along with a grant of $20,000 from the Youngstown Foundation, a local grantmaking organization. The Ursuline community's newsletter pointed out that the project was launched after "area leaders in both the public and private sectors expressed to the Ursuline Sisters the need in our community for safe, adequate, affordable housing for senior citizens of more moderate incomes."

On September 15, 2013, the public and media were invited to an open house for Ursuline Sisters Senior Living, and visitors were impressed by the architectural work completed by Youngstown-based BSHM Architects.[296]

The final phase of the project involved the renovation of the motherhouse's healthcare wing, which was reconfigured to provide ten healthcare suites, a kitchen, support spaces and an all-seasons porch, all of which were handicapped accessible. The upgraded wing features central air-conditioning and a large physical therapy room with state-of-the-art equipment. The revamping of the healthcare wing reflects the Ursulines' desire to keep older sisters at the motherhouse as long as possible.[297]

Not surprisingly, Ursuline associates participated in the reconfiguration project. Peggy Eicher, in her effort to maintain the motherhouse grounds, already managed a team of workers comprising volunteers and day reporters. In 2011, when construction on the motherhouse commenced, many of those workers participated in the preliminary demolition of former living quarters. "The contract indicated that we would gut the wings that were scheduled to undergo construction," Eicher explained.

When Eicher retired as the motherhouse's director of operations in 2019, she continued as director of Ursuline Sisters Senior Living. While the apartments have become a source of income for the religious community, Eicher emphasized that they also serve as an important ministry. "If you look around at the average rents for one-bedroom or two-bedroom apartments in Canfield, Austintown, and Boardman Townships, you'll see that our rents are wonderfully reasonable," Eicher said. "Apart from that, residents benefit from programming that builds a sense of community."[298]

Ursuline associate Bonnie Arditi, a hairdresser and former caregiver, moved into a one-bedroom apartment at the motherhouse in 2021, not long after the death of her elderly mother. Her initial concerns about feeling isolated were quickly dispelled. "I'm never alone," Arditi insisted. "All residents have access to the pool and wellness programs. On Saturday mornings, we have yoga and stretching classes. We have a back patio that's very welcoming, and we sit out there and have lunch together....It's a real community."[299]

Eicher confirmed Arditi's description of the welcoming atmosphere at Ursuline Sisters Senior Living. "It's great to see how people who never knew each other in the past have come together to help one another," she said. Eicher pointed out that demand for apartments is so high that some prospective residents have been on a waiting list for three years. "Our residents are aged fifty-five and above, and nobody is leaving," she added.

In 2017, six new apartments were built on the second floor of the far west wing of the motherhouse. More recently, an additional three were built on the near west side of the building, bringing the total number of rentable apartments to twenty. Eicher indicated that a twenty-first apartment, known as the Pilgrim Suite, is available to rent for out-of-town guests and speakers.

Reaching Out to Younger Adults

While the Ursuline associate program has bolstered the community's ministries, leaders recognized a need to reach out to younger people. Starting in 2011, the Ursuline Sisters made a strategic effort to engage young adults through service and learning opportunities, including internships and alternative spring breaks.

The core team responsible for developing the program included Sister Norma Raupple, Sister Nancy Pawlen and Sister Therese Ann Rich, as well as Ursuline associates Ray Novotny and Michele Ristich Gatts.

Working with Baltimore-based Notre Dame Mission Volunteers (NDMV), a faith-based nonprofit established in 1992 by the Sisters of Notre Dame de Namur, the Ursuline community secured the participation of service-oriented college graduates seeking on-the-job experience.

In 1995, NDMV established a partnership with AmeriCorps, an independent government agency that supports stipend-based volunteer programs throughout the country.

Among other things, AmeriCorps members who worked with the Ursulines in the fields of education and social services developed and implemented curricula for immigrant families in English language learning and other basic skills instructions. "We have changed with the times, and we've stayed positive with our aging," observed Sister Norma Raupple, who currently oversees the young adult outreach ministry. "The future is necessarily going to involve a mix of people...including younger associates."

Sister Norma explained that the program for young adults involves the recruitment of scores of volunteers from Ursuline and Mooney High Schools, regional public high schools and several universities in northeastern Ohio and western Pennsylvania.

In recent years, she has also worked to maintain relationships with young adults who previously volunteered with the Ursuline Sisters through AmeriCorps. "They want an ongoing relationship with us, but when they get married or move away, the proximity is no longer there," Sister Norma explained. "But if some of those families were to form the nucleus of a community that maintained contact with us, who knows what could happen?"[300]

In 2016, the religious community established Angela's Villa, a gathering place that provides opportunities for service, prayer and community to young women serving in ministry with the Ursuline Sisters.

Sister Norma Raupple (*top right*) resides at Angela's Villa, which provides opportunities for service, prayer and community for young women serving in ministry. *Courtesy of Ursuline Sisters of Youngstown.*

Sister Norma indicated the donation of the house that became Angela's Villa was negotiated by Scott Schulick, a Canfield-based financial advisor. At the time, Schulick, who is also an Ursuline associate, served as trustee for a woman who wanted to donate her property to a worthy cause. "When he showed us the home, it definitely had possibilities," Sister Norma explained, "and we were thrilled when he and his business partner offered it to us."

From there, Ursuline associate Peggy Eicher, who still served at that time as the motherhouse's director of operations, assembled a team of volunteers to refurbish the house. Within two weeks, a new roof and windows had been installed at the home, while volunteers refinished dining room furniture and scrubbed kitchen cabinets.

Meanwhile, the interior was repainted, while new carpeting and a new shower were installed. "The beautifully upgraded rooms work well for our gathering spaces," Sister Norma noted. "I reside there, and the young women are creating ways to come together to build community and support each other."

Sister Norma added that each month, the women share a Sunday brunch after attending mass at a nearby parish. To ensure that the young women involved in the ministry stay informed, the Young Adult Committee maintains a blog called *Voices from Angela's Villa*.[301]

Enlisting the Help of Active Professionals

Meanwhile, the Ursuline Sisters have sought to engage professionals who remain active in their careers. A good example can be found in the involvement of Scott Schulick, who negotiated the donation of the house that serves as Angela's Villa.

Like many Ursuline associates, Schulick's introduction to the religious community occurred in a classroom. "When I enrolled as a freshman at Ursuline High School in 1986, there were at least eight sisters on the staff," he recalled. "So, the Ursuline presence still permeated the school's culture."

Schulick admitted that before enrolling at the center city high school, he rarely ventured beyond Youngstown's relatively insulated west side. "The student body at Ursuline ran the whole socioeconomic gamut," he recalled. "There were very wealthy kids and very poor kids.…You came away with the idea that we're all part of God's family, all part of this human experience."

The social justice values Schulick absorbed at the school would complement the practical skills he developed later in the areas of business and finance. After enrolling as a business major at Youngstown State University, Schulick pondered a career as either a stockbroker or financial advisor. "Shortly after graduating, I was lucky enough to secure a job with Butler, Wick and Company (now Stifel Nicolaus and Company)," he explained. "It all worked out—I got to go to work in the industry I wanted, in the city I wanted, and with a venerable local institution."

As a young financial advisor seeking clients, Schulick understood that community involvement positioned him to interact with people of influence. At the same time, he viewed these activities as a civic responsibility. "Ursuline High School instilled a service-oriented perspective in its students," he said. "So, I carried that with me. While it was beneficial to my business to be engaged in the community, I also became involved in projects that were meaningful to me."

Schulick began his journey in 2012, when one of his clients, Marilyn Rheil, encouraged him to join the associates program. Rheil, an Ursuline associate and longtime benefactor of the religious community, suggested that he contact Sister Norma Raupple about participating in the program's formation process.

In retrospect, Schulick found the experience deepened his understanding of the religious community. "The formation period focused on the life and ministry of St. Angela Merici," he explained. "Her story sheds light on the evolution of the Ursulines. It's clear they're living up to her teaching to change with the times."

Around this time, Sister Regina Rogers, then completing her six-year term as general superior, invited Schulick to serve on the board of the Ursuline Center, a move that paved the way for additional leadership roles with the Ursuline Sisters.[302]

Over the years, other professionals have shared their gifts with the community. Like Scott Schulick, Dan Wakefield, a veteran educator, established a relationship with the sisters when he was still a high school student. During his senior year at Ursuline High School, Wakefield was recruited to work at the motherhouse by Sister Kathleen McCarragher, then the director of operations.

After graduating from high school, Wakefield continued to work at the motherhouse while completing a bachelor's degree in education at Youngstown State University. One of his first classes at YSU was a foundations course that included fifteen hours of required tutoring, and he was surprised to learn that he had been assigned to the children's program of the Ursulines' HIV/AIDS ministry.

The program, known as Casa Madre, was relatively new, and Wakefield admitted that he was nervous about the assignment. "I knew nothing about HIV/AIDS, and I had no experience working with children in poverty or city youth," he explained. Nevertheless, he enjoyed the experience and agreed to volunteer for the remainder of the term. "When that term ended, the director asked me to work part time at Casa Madre," he recalled.

Over the next four years, Wakefield's activities brought him into regular contact with Sister Kathleen Minchin, the director of the community's HIV/AIDS ministry, and Brigid Kennedy, who served as the associate director. He also worked closely with the Cleveland Ursulines who then staffed Casa Madre: Sister Susan Durkin and Sister Susan Zion.

After graduating from YSU, Wakefield accepted a position teaching history at an elementary school in East Las Vegas, Nevada, a job he enjoyed.

Participants in a community day include (*left to right*) Sister Martha Reed, Sister Nancy DiCola, Sister Pauline Dalpe and Sister Helen Shea. *Courtesy of Ursuline Sisters of Youngstown.*

However, in 2007, he learned that two of his older relatives were experiencing health problems, and he chose to return to the Mahoning Valley.

At that point, Sister Kathleen and Kennedy offered him two part-time jobs with the community's HIV/AIDS ministry, and for the next year, Wakefield divided his time between reception duties at the clinic and teaching at Casa Madre. In 2008, after accepting a full-time job at an online charter school, he spent six years balancing his teaching responsibilities with his volunteer work at Casa Madre and the Guardian Angel Café.

Then in 2014, Kennedy, now the codirector of the HIV/AIDS ministry, offered Wakefield a full-time administrative post with the ministry. He learned that Sister Kathleen was planning to step back from some of her responsibilities, while the ministry was also securing grants for a housing program that required additional staff support.

As a special projects coordinator, Wakefield helped launch the community's annual Nun Run, a fundraiser that would benefit the HIV/AIDS ministry's children's program over the next eight years. The fundraiser included a one-mile walk, a five-mile race and a child-friendly competition known as the Kids' Fun Run.

Wakefield was appointed as the interim director of the Ursulines' HIV/ AIDS ministry in 2016. Sister Kathleen had decided to retire, and Kennedy had accepted another leadership role with the community. Finally, in November 2017, Wakefield was named director, a position he held until August 2021.

An Ursuline associate since 2013, Wakefield is a full-time instructor in teacher education at Youngstown's Eastern Gateway Community College and part-time instructor at Youngstown State University. Nevertheless, he remains active as a volunteer in programs including Dorothy Day House of Hospitality. "The most rewarding experience for me has been getting out there and being with people who are different than me," he stated. "The Ursulines always showed me how to interact with people with attitudes of respect and compassion and hospitality."[303]

REORGANIZING A RELIGIOUS COMMUNITY

Despite the religious community's mounting challenges, the Ursuline Sisters continued to exert a positive influence on the Youngstown area through such ministries as Beatitude House, Ursuline Sisters HIV/AIDS, Ursuline Preschool and Kindergarten, Ursuline Sisters Senior Living and the Ursuline Center's various adult education, health and wellness programs. "While local companies have come and gone, the Ursulines' presence in the Valley remains strong and continues to grow," stated an article that appeared in the Youngstown-based *Business Journal* in November 2017. "They have ministries that in some way touch all lives, but their focus is on helping the poor and disadvantaged, especially women and children."

To guarantee a continuation of these ministries, the Ursulines initiated steps toward the end of 2016 to establish a nonprofit corporation. "This strategic plan will ensure that our ministries…have the structure and leadership in place to continue their vital missions—not only for the present but the long-term," explained Sister Mary McCormick, who began her first term as general superior in 2014.

The nonprofit, known as Ursuline Ministries, was led by Brigid Kennedy, who served as the organization's president. "I know how life-giving and transforming those ministries are and all the places the Ursulines have served and can continue to serve for the Mahoning Valley," Kennedy observed at the time.

Kennedy explained that in her role as president, she would consult with a board of directors that included Sister Mary, board chair; Ursuline

In 2019, more than thirty-five Ursuline Sisters gathered for a group portrait in the motherhouse chapel. *Courtesy of Ursuline Sisters of Youngstown.*

Sisters Leadership Team councilors Sister Patricia McNicholas, Sister Regina Rogers and Sister Norma Raupple; Frank Dixon, a certified public accountant; Patricia Fleming, a retired principal of Ursuline High School; and Mary Beth Houser, an attorney.[304]

More recently, Kennedy indicated that the primary challenge facing Ursuline Ministries (now Ursuline Sisters Mission) was bringing the religious community's mission into the future as the number of sisters continued to decline. "What we're trying to do is prepare for the impact of decreasing numbers, as the sisters' capacity for administration diminishes over time," she noted. "Our goal is to arrange things so that the sisters can focus on those activities that are important to them as a religious community and not worry so much about the administrative and operational side of things."[305]

For Sister Mary, the community's decision to restructure reflected its willingness to embrace the realities of the future. "When I assumed leadership in 2014, our ministries were separate corporations, and all were administered by nuns," she explained. "It didn't take much analysis to determine that this situation wasn't going to last long, since the person running that corporation was probably going to be the last sister to serve as its administrator."

She noted that by the time the nonprofit corporation was launched in 2017, the community had already begun the process of installing laypeople in positions of authority once held by sisters. "At this point, we don't have a single sister who serves as the chief operating officer of a ministry," Sister Mary noted. "At the same time, we take comfort in the fact that these ministries are being administered by competent and gifted laypeople."[306]

PREPARING FOR A PANDEMIC

A test for the Ursulines' new leadership team came with the onset of the COVID-19 pandemic, which precipitated a national public health emergency. While Ohio's governor Mike DeWine was lauded in some quarters for enacting a statewide lockdown as early as March 2020, the Ursuline Sisters had been preparing for the emergency weeks beforehand. "We brought together key people and discussed what we knew, what we didn't know, and some important questions that needed to be addressed," Kennedy recalled.

These questions dealt with issues that ranged from client food insecurity to infection control to the sourcing of supplies. On March 16, 2020, when Governor DeWine and Ohio Department of Health director Amy Acton held a press conference announcing sweeping public safety measures, the Ursulines swung into action.

In the period of uncertainty that came before the wide availability of vaccines, the religious community took proactive steps to preserve the health of the sisters, especially those who were older. "We've had an incredible amount of success," Kennedy observed. "Unfortunately, that's not true of many other religious communities or other communal living settings."

Precautions at the motherhouse included a suspension of activities (including land and water exercise classes), the compulsory wearing of masks in public areas of the motherhouse and a suspension of face-to-face meetings in favor of telehealth calls and Zoom sessions. An unexpected outcome of the pandemic was the role that many sisters played in comforting area residents through messages disseminated by phone, on social media and in newsletters.[307]

As the Ursulines emerged from the trauma of the pandemic, their leaders would place a greater emphasis on employee wellness initiatives. "Prior to COVID, we had begun to enhance employee development, including more focus on trauma-informed care and strengths-based growth," Kennedy observed. "We initiated an employee assistance program, engaged consultants, and used counselors in our clinic, school

Brigid Kennedy (*left*), the president and CEO of Ursuline Sisters Mission, cooperates with Sister Mary McCormick, the general superior, to oversee the community's ministries. *Courtesy of Ursuline Sisters of Youngstown.*

and outreach programs." She pointed out that the pandemic "heightened the need for all these offerings."[308] More substantial changes were in the wings.

In early 2023, the Ursulines announced yet another restructuring of their ministries. Ursuline Ministries, rebranded as Ursuline Sisters Missions (USM), now featured shared service teams for finance, human resources, development and mission/equity/resilience. "Instead of each ministry managing those functions separately, these teams now share resources, working across all ministries," explained Kennedy, who serves as the president and CEO of Ursuline Sisters Mission. In a streamlining of services, USM absorbed education outreach programs, including Ursuline Sisters Scholars and Immigrant Outreach (formerly under Beatitude House), as well as the HIV/AIDS Ministry and Beatitude House.

Kennedy added that plans were being developed to ensure that aging sisters with chronic health issues could remain at the motherhouse as long as possible. "Our draft plan involves converting the sisters' current living space, plus some other areas in the motherhouse, to assisted living suites for the sisters and others, generating important supportive income," she stated. "This will allow the sisters to remain at home at the motherhouse longer, expand staffing, and keep the building available for sisters and the ministries."[309]

A TANGIBLE LEGACY

Reports of the restructuring of the Ursulines' ministries overlapped with bittersweet news for dozens of local families, as the religious community announced the imminent closure of Ursuline Preschool and Kindergarten. Founded in 1963, the preschool opened at the time of the motherhouse's completion and had since served thousands of children.

By the start of the 2022–23 academic year, however, the community's leadership team recognized that the income received through tuition no longer covered the school's expenses. "This subsidy has been provided in a variety of ways: through a very modest stipend paid to sisters, little rent payment for the use of the facility which the Ursuline Sisters built, and in recent years, improving wages and benefits for teachers and assistants," explained Sister Mary McCormick, the Ursulines' general superior. "The Ursuline Sisters are no longer able to shoulder this expense."

Sister Mary added that when the school first opened its doors six decades earlier, "there were no comparable preschool programs in the area." By the time the preschool announced that it would close, however, at least five local Catholic parishes operated early childhood learning centers.

The general superior praised the school's religious and lay staff members for their years of dedication and thanked parents for "entrusting their children to the care of Ursuline Preschool and Kindergarten."[310]

In a sense, Ursuline Preschool's closure represented the final stage in the religious community's shift away from classroom teaching. By 2023, Ursuline nuns were no longer present in local parish and diocesan school classrooms. Moreover, Ursuline High School, the iconic institution the order had established back in 1905, retained not a single Ursuline Sister on its teaching staff or administration.

Still, the legacy of those accumulated years of guidance and instruction remains tangible. John Ulicney, who taught biology at Ursuline High School for forty-six years before his retirement, observed that the Ursulines, as religious educators, distinguished themselves by their accessibility. "While they had strong professional values, they were always approachable," Ulicney noted. "They could joke and kid with you, and they extended that kind of openness to their students. To this day, alumni are quick to identify as Ursuline graduates, which reflects the strong tie they still have with the Ursuline Sisters."[311]

Meanwhile, Scott Schulick, who graduated from Ursuline High School in 1990, pointed out that despite the absence of Ursuline nuns on the staff, the school actively promotes the values that the community represents. "Through the work of Dr. Linda Miller, a retired teacher and active Ursuline associate, the school has embraced the charism of St. Angela Merici…and that's been a wonderful connection," Schulick said. "In the past, we didn't necessarily focus as much on St. Angela. This new development has been a strong boost for the culture of the school, and it strengthens the connection with the Ursuline Sisters."[312]

He indicated that the high school's current staff includes Ursuline associates Nicky and Mark Uerling, as well as Cindy Lacko and Lisa Devlin. He added that another associate, Aimee Morrison, retired as a teacher at the end of the 2022–23 academic year.

Sister Jerome Corcoran (*left*) greets philanthropist Dr. Rashid Abdu at an event celebrating students involved in Sister Jerome's Scholars, a program known today as Ursuline Sisters Scholars. *Courtesy of Ursuline Sisters of Youngstown.*

For Father Richard Murphy, the school's current president, the Ursuline Sisters' values played an important role in shaping the institution's curriculum over the decades. Father Murphy, whose father graduated from the school in 1936, grew up leafing through old yearbooks—and one image stuck with him. "In those yearbooks, you'll find two ribbon banners underneath the Ursuline Sisters' educational crest," he explained. "The first, of course, shows their motto: *Soli Deo Gloria*, or 'For the Glory of God Alone.' Beneath that you'll find a rather large ribbon banner containing a phrase from the Book of Daniel, also rendered in Latin: 'Those who instruct the many to justice will shine as stars for all eternity.' To me, this reflects a commitment to an education for justice, as well as a conscious adherence to values."

The priest suggested that the Ursuline Sisters carried that motto forward when they made the collective decision to educate working-class boys. "Here, in the heart of a harsh economy and the midst of a blue-collar community, they took on a ministry for the poor rather early on—and one without limit."[313]

Other observers have called attention to the religious community's flexibility in the face of changing circumstances. Monsignor Jay Clarke, a retired priest, applauded the Ursulines for their creative response to such challenges as falling vocations and a decline in the number of Catholic schools. "The sisters themselves began to recognize that there were options beyond teaching in schools," Monsignor Clarke observed. "Now, the Ursuline Sisters have many alternatives that are still within the spirit of their charism but were not thought of before the 1960s."[314]

Similarly, Father Edward Noga, pastor emeritus at Youngstown's Saint Patrick Parish, suggested that the Ursulines' development has reflected their astute reading of religious and social trends. "The Ursulines have expanded their mission in a way that parallels the Church's tremendous expansion of its larger mission, in terms of witness value," Father Noga said. "The Ursulines have also been proactive in making sure the ministries they have now are going to be well-run, well-funded, and benefit from good leadership in the future."[315]

Meanwhile, civic leaders across the Mahoning Valley have characterized the Ursuline Sisters as a force for good. H. William Lawson, the executive director of the Mahoning Valley Historical Society, highlighted the Ursulines' role as innovators who are not afraid to address potentially divisive topics. "In the last forty years, they've pursued ministries that move beyond parishes and into the social service network of our community," Lawson observed.

Sister Patricia McNicholas (*left*) poses with young adult volunteers at Beatitude House, a nonprofit organization for homeless single mothers. *Courtesy of Ursuline Sisters of Youngstown.*

"They've taken up issues that are controversial, while embracing and ministering to those who have been ostracized by mainstream society."[316]

Lawson's wife, Joan Reedy Lawson, who currently serves as the chancellor and archivist of the Diocese of Youngstown, called attention to the ways in which the order has navigated a social environment that is less accommodating to institutional religion. "The societal move away from organized religion is a challenge," she acknowledged. "In response, however, they're nurturing love and mercy among those who aren't always open to organized religion. Yet serving in a way that reflects the message of the gospel is still spreading the gospel. Whether or not a millennial wants to participate in organized religion, she or he is still going to want to participate in those values. The fact that the Ursulines can exert this kind of positive influence without turning people away is truly a grace."[317]

Envisioning the Future

As Sister Mary McCormick reflected on the order's future, she recalled that when she joined the Ursuline Sisters in 1975, the community was undergoing changes that would become more pronounced over time. "I was one of those for whom entering was a completely different experience," she observed. "When I entered, few women were drawn to religious life, and the last person to have entered before I was Sr. Regina Rogers—and that had been seven years earlier."

Unlike Sister Mary, however, Sister Regina had been part of a large class that contracted unexpectedly when her classmates pursued other options. This dramatic decline in vocations resulted in an easing of the formality that permeated the pre–Vatican II era.

When Sister Mary entered, the community's novitiate had been moved from the motherhouse to the convent at Saint Nicholas Parish in Struthers, and the Ursulines no longer enjoyed a relationship with the local university that enabled them to hold classes at the motherhouse.

Meanwhile, Sister Mary, a nineteen-year-old sophomore at YSU, was encouraged to interact with novices connected to other Ursuline communities, as well as those associated with the Sisters of the Humility of Mary, the Sisters of Saint Joseph and the Dominican Sisters. These orders, after all, were working together to negotiate a radically altered religious environment.

If her formation period reflected traditional structures dictated by canon law, she was nevertheless entering a community for which everything had changed. "It was a time of renewing religious life in light of the modern world in which we lived," Sister Mary explained. "That was a specific mandate of Vatican II, and it was accomplished, in part, by moving novices from the motherhouse to a smaller community, by having them attend classes at a university, and by introducing them to what were called inter-congregational formation programs."

Some things had not changed, however. "The presumption, for the most part, was that I would probably be a teacher, without anyone overtly saying so," she recalled. "That was still the mindset."

Yet even in this regard, the ground was beginning to shift. "The Church, overall, was coming to the realization that there were new ministries," Sister Mary explained. "If you want someone to serve as director of religious education—not simply run the school program—you need to determine who is trained and who is available."

Dr. Helen K. Lafferty (*fourth from left*), the interim president of Youngstown State University, pays a visit to the Ursuline Motherhouse. Dr. Lafferty, a former Ursuline Sister, reconnected with (*left to right*) Sister Patricia McNicholas, Sister Norma Raupple, Sister Regina Rogers, Sister Mary McCormick and Sister Mary Alyce Koval. *Courtesy of Ursuline Sisters of Youngstown.*

Bishops and pastors alike concluded that the Ursuline Sisters, with their strong academic credentials, were up to the job. Sister Mary—whose qualifications include a PhD in contemporary systematic theology from Fordham University and a graduate degree in religious education from Loyola University of New Orleans—exemplifies this pattern.

A committed educator, Sister Mary now serves as a professor of systematic theology and the academic dean at Saint Mary Seminary and Graduate School of Theology for the Diocese of Cleveland, where she trains young men who are studying for the priesthood.

In the years since Sister Mary joined the community, many of the parish schools the Ursulines once staffed have disappeared, and those sisters who remain active have shifted to other ministries. Where some might perceive symptoms of decline, however, Sister Mary finds evidence of renewal, as her community is moving closer to Saint Angela Merici's vision of a body of laypeople working in the community to address the needs of the times.[318]

For Brigid Kennedy, the president and CEO of Ursuline Sisters Mission, members of the religious community are trailblazers in a church that is regularly challenged to become more socially engaged. "The sisters are very orthodox, clearly, but they have the freedom to be present to people in a way in which the traditional church hasn't always succeeded," she said. "Over the years, the sisters have brought the Church to the people, instead of expecting those people to show up at the church door. They cut through many of the empty formalities in which the Church often gets caught up—and that's a big part of their legacy."

Like Sister Mary, Kennedy expressed confidence that the Ursuline Sisters' mission would be passed on. "It's not about how many sisters there are, or how many are working in parishes or schools or other types of ministries," she stated. "It's about what they represent and how they've empowered future generations to do the same thing. The community has embraced, whether explicitly or unconsciously, the idea that we're all given gifts that we need to share with the community. We don't have to build infrastructure. We don't need to have our names on buildings. Our legacy is reflected in the people we touch."[319]

This sense of mission has been coupled with a clear-eyed view of the future that has inspired the Ursulines to engage in constant planning. Father Robert Bonnot, who often says mass at the motherhouse chapel, is aware of significant changes within the religious community. "What I notice is that the chapel is rarely full because you have a lot of nuns living out on their own, which is more consistent with St. Angela's intentions," he stated. "But the fact is, you also see signs of aging. Little by little, the Ursulines are withering away as a religious community."

Father Bonnot acknowledged, however, that the community has taken active steps to preserve its ministry. "The other side of that situation is that they have brilliantly developed an effective program of associates," he noted. "That's probably going to be the future of the Ursulines and their ministry."

Yet Father Bonnot hesitated to dismiss the possibility that religious life would resurface at some point. "There won't necessarily be huge convents with hundreds of sisters moving around," he observed. "On the other hand, you will see people of deep faith who are committed to projects that meet the needs of the community, and they're going to go out and pursue them."[320]

As a student of history, Sister Mary is aware of the unanticipated events that shaped the development of the Ursuline Sisters of Youngstown. "There's a lot of literature out there that suggests we're living in an axial age in which everything is changing," she stated. "That's especially true of religious life."

While Sister Mary expressed confidence that the community's network of supporters would help preserve its ministries, she also held out hope that the Ursuline Sisters would reemerge in a new form. "Part of being hopeful about the future is to ask how we can continue to be faithful to religious life, so that this sense of fidelity resonates for others down the road," she noted.

Sister Mary indicated that a lesson can be drawn from the story of the Ursuline Sisters of Boulogne-sur-Mer, a religious community that

Attendees at a Beach Boys concert in Youngstown include (*left to right*) Sister Mary Alyce Koval, Pattie Condello, a diocesan pastoral associate; Sister Marie Maravola; Sister Norma Raupple; Sister Nancy Pawlen; Sister Regina Rogers; Sister Carole Suhar; and Sister Darla Jean Vogelsang. *Courtesy of Ursuline Sisters of Youngstown.*

was targeted by France's revolutionary government in the late eighteenth century. "After the French Revolution, this community was defunct for a hundred years," Sister Mary explained. "I'm sure that many people at the time believed they were living in a period of terrible despair. Then someone remembered their story, and the order rebounded."

Indeed, in 1850, Bishop Amadeus Rappe, Cleveland's first episcopal leader, persuaded that same French order to send a group of sisters to his new diocese. Fourteen years later, in 1874, the Cleveland community bishop Rappe fostered sent six nuns to Youngstown to staff a local parish school. "The story of the Ursuline Sisters of Boulogne-sur-Mer is therefore linked to our own history," Sister Mary observed. "Now, here we are—about 275 years later—in a new world with a very different way of life. Who knows what the future will bring?"[321]

URSULINE SISTERS OF YOUNGSTOWN, 1874–2023

1. M. Agnes Gilday
2. M. Ursula Croxton
3. M. Theresa McMahon
4. M. Stanislaus Rudge
5. M. Felix Polion
6. M. Rose Connolly
7. M. Louis Pautot
8. M. Berchmans Kniesel
9. M. Anastasia Connolly
10. M. Stanislaus Mulhern
11. M. Ann Hayes
12. M. Clare McMahon
13. M. Scholastica Canavan
14. M. Angela Brown
15. M. James Sullivan
16. M. John Radnor
17. M. Incarnation Lacy
18. M. Aloysius McAndrews
19. M. Carmel Santangelo
20. M. Rita Trundley
21. M. Gertrude Forristall

22. M. Ann Cullie
23. Sacred Heart Griffin
24. Florence Gilboy
25. Alice Marie Byrne
26. M. Isabel Morrison
27. M. Augustine Edwards
28. M. Barbara Burford
29. M. Magdalene Creagan
30. Blessed Sacrament Whelan
31. Magdalene de Pazzi Mundie
32. Mother M. Lawrence McCaffrey
33. Francis de Sales Cassidy
34. M. Cecilia Wernet
35. Mother M. Joseph Hopkins
36. Mother M. Agnes Ryan
37. M. Columba Gettins
38. M. Xavier Rudge
39. M. Ursula Hopkins
40. M. Ignatius Gerrity
41. M. Rita Krispinsky
42. Mother M. Bernard McCann
43. M. Alphonsus McCabe
44. M. Patricia Fitzgerald
45. M. Rose Striegal
46. M. Celestine Duffy
47. M. Eugene Huggins
48. M. Camillus Creagan
49. M. Catherine Mundie
50. M. Anthony McGill
51. M. Leo Kelly
52. M. Norbert Reilly
53. M. Evangelista Mahony
54. M. Gertrude Jancar
55. M. Theresa Moran
56. M. Francis Carroll
57. M. Genevieve Kelly
58. M. Agatha Scanlon
59. M. Brendan Grimes
60. M. Malachi Burke

61. M. Helen Wernet
62. M. Clare Lynaugh
63. M. Benedict Gorman
64. Margaret Mary McCabe
65. Mother M. Vincent O'Connell
66. M. Methodia Thurik
67. Mother M. Paul Townley
68. Mother Holy Angels Laughlin
69. M. Dominica Gaspic
70. M. Laurentina Butler
71. M. Dolores Waidman
72. M. Charles Hoffman
73. M. Irene Breen
74. M. Martha Eurell
75. Marie Therese Illencik
76. M. Damian Reilly
77. M. Philomena Hric
78. M. Dorothy Leslie
79. M. Beatrice Madden
80. Roseanne Gerrity
81. M. Regina Schneider
82. Carmelita Lorenzo
83. M. Coletta Braun
84. Anastasia Ryan
85. Mary Angela Gilboy
86. Mary Ellen O'Connell
87. Stanislaus Oravec
88. M. Veronica Labuda
89. Margaret Fitzgerald
90. Loretta Riles
91. Barbara Turk
92. Anna Marie Saunders
93. M. Aloysius Fahy
94. Magdalene Ganofsky
95. M. Florence Mulhall
96. M. Patrice Connolly
97. Cyril Friedman
98. M. Dorothea Cavanaugh
99. Evelyn Croell

100. Eileen Kelly
101. Mildred Gilboy
102. Roberta Petrose
103. Mother Edna Marie Brindle
104. Perpetua White
105. Helen Therese Tesner
106. Monica Ruby
107. Carmel Incarnato
108. Kathleen Kelly
109. Mary Alice Ryan
110. Mary Louise McGraw
111. Alberta Gerlach
112. Mary Grace Daley
113. Marie Joseph Ritchie
114. Mary Esther Stoltz
115. Janet Elaine Walsh
116. Geraldine Stanislaw
117. Christine Carroll
118. Joan Gerlach
119. Imelda Maloney
120. Winifred Melody
121. Augustine Yuhas
122. Agnes Marie Beil
123. Blanche Klempay
124. Madeleine McNally
125. Mary Agnes Convery
126. M. Ruth Kupec
127. Catherine Calvey
128. Ann Mary Thurik
129. M. Lucille Onda
130. Marie Hughes
131. Bernadette Gezic
132. Elizabeth Kupec
133. Charlotte McEvoy
134. Francis de Sales McDade
135. Marie Antoinette Shipka
136. Raymond Manley
137. Anna Marie Manley
138. Immaculata Carroll

139. Bernadine Fickers
140. Elizabeth Kerrigan
141. Patrick McIlduff
142. LaVerne Weinheimer
143. Mary Conroy
144. Jean Marie Eskay
145. Anne Lynch
146. Alice Marie Morley
147. Marie Celeste Stanislaw
148. Mary John Bertaldo
149. Rosemary Deibel
150. Marie Celine Olejar
151. Jacquelyn Herpy
152. Margaret Scheetz
153. Rita DeChello
154. Gabriel Manley
155. Mary Volk
156. Cecilia Morano
157. Juliana Barrett
158. Ursula Marie Illencik
159. Bernice Bosanac
160. Edith Weir
161. Martina Casey
162. Shirley Getz
163. Ellen Rose Donovan
164. Mary Catherine Doran
165. Mary William Yurko
166. Virginia McDermott
167. Albert Marie Beil
168. Carol Ann Higgins
169. Victoria Pascarella
170. Miriam Engles
171. Teresa Winsen
172. Marie Helene Chismar
173. Lois Walter
174. Marcia Welsh
175. Elizabeth Ann Schuster
176. Julia Baluch
177. Brendan Sherlock

178. Helen Shea
179. Judith Shoff
180. Mary Dunn
181. Janet Frantz
182. Gertrude Paris
183. Mary Lee Nalley
184. Mary O'Leary
185. Germaine Staron
186. Rose Dailey
187. Frances Marie Sopko
188. Eleanor Santangelo
189. Jerome Corcoran
190. Jeanne Cigolle
191. Therese Ann Rich
192. Mary Ellen Dean
193. Isabel Rudge
194. Mary Ann Coz
195. Pauline Dalpe
196. Nancy Dawson
197. Nancy DiCola
198. Mary Ann Diersing
199. Elizabeth Anne Freidhoff
200. Jan Gier
201. Marilyn Hoover
202. Charlotte Italiano
203. Eileen Kernan
204. Mary Alyce Koval
205. Dorothy Kundracik
206. Janice Kusick
207. Marlene LoGrasso
208. Marie Maravola
209. Kathleen McCarragher
210. Mary McCormick
211. Patricia McNicholas
212. Kathleen Minchin
213. Bridget Nolan
214. Helen Nordick
215. Nancy Pawlen
216. Carole Suhar

217. Norma Raupple
218. Martha Reed
219. Regina Rogers
220. Diane Toth
221. Darla Jean Vogelsang

NOTES

Introduction

1. *Youngstown Vindicator*, December 15, 1963.
2. *Centennial of Service*.
3. *Steel Valley News*, May 18, 1964.
4. *Youngstown Vindicator*, January 10, 1960.
5. *Youngstown Vindicator*, July 14, 1961.

Chapter 1

6. *Youngstown Daily Vindicator*, October 4, 1878.
7. Leonard, "Ethnic Tensions," 394.
8. Gabert, *In Hoc Signo?*, 46.
9. Mahoney, *A Tree in the Valley*, 33–34.
10. Lynch and Dean, "Where We've Been," 7.
11. "Entertainment for the Benefit of Ursuline Sisters."
12. Mahoney, *A Tree in the Valley*, 32–33.
13. *Youngstown Telegram*, May 3, 1919.
14. Gross, *War Against Catholicism*, 2.
15. Ledochowska, *Angela Merici*, 1:11.
16. Ibid., 13.
17. Ibid., 16.

18. Ibid., 27.
19. Ibid., 23.
20. Ibid., 32.
21. Ibid., 33.
22. Ibid., 60–61.
23. Ibid., 66.
24. Ibid., ix.
25. Ibid., 87–88.
26. Ibid., 111.
27. Buser, *Also in Your Midst*, 9.
28. Lynch and Dean, "Where We've Been," 2.
29. Ibid., 2–3.
30. *Youngstown Telegram*, December 17, 1924.
31. Lynch and Dean, "Where We've Been," 7.
32. *Youngstown Daily Vindicator*, July 3, 1895.
33. *Youngstown Vindicator*, January 22, 1933.
34. *Youngstown Vindicator*, September 29, 1957.
35. *Youngstown Vindicator*, January 22, 1933.
36. "Seventy-Fifth Anniversary of St. Ann's Church."
37. Lynch and Dean, "Where We've Been," 9–10.
38. *Youngstown Telegram*, December 17, 1924.
39. *Youngstown Daily Vindicator*, February 15, 1897.

Chapter 2

40. Blue, Jenkins, Lawson and Reedy, *Mahoning Memories*, 76.
41. Ibid., 94.
42. *Youngstown Telegram*, March 7, 1930.
43. "Cathedral Parish of St. Columba," 9.
44. *Youngstown Vindicator*, June 4, 1972.
45. "Cathedral Parish of St. Columba," 8.
46. Lynch and Dean, "Where We've Been," 11–12.
47. *Ursuline High School Jubilee, 1905–1980.*
48. Lynch and Dean, "Where We've Been," 11–12.
49. *Youngstown Telegram*, May 3, 1919.
50. *Youngstown Vindicator*, November 24, 1974.
51. "New Ursuline High School."

52. *Ursuline High School Jubilee, 1905–1980.*
53. Lynch and Dean, "Where We've Been," 12.
54. Rudge, interviews.
55. *Ursuline High School Jubilee, 1905–1980.*
56. Lynch and Dean, "Where We've Been," 13.
57. Rudge, interviews.
58. Lynch and Dean, "Where We've Been," 13.
59. Rudge, interviews.
60. Lynch and Dean, "Where We've Been," 13.
61. *Ursuline High School Jubilee, 1905–1980.*
62. McFadden, *March of the Eucharist*, 22.
63. *Youngstown Telegram*, March 7, 1930.
64. *Youngstown Vindicator*, December 7, 1925.
65. *Youngstown Telegram*, October 23, 1925.
66. *Youngstown Vindicator*, September 4, 1937.
67. *Youngstown Vindicator*, June 11, 1950.
68. *High Gear*, March 1958, 7.
69. *Youngstown Vindicator*, June 6, 1943.
70. *Youngstown Vindicator*, June 6, 1943.
71. Lynch and Dean, "Where We've Been," 27.
72. "Youngstown Ursulines: Significant Dates," 1–3.
73. *Youngstown Vindicator*, May 5, 1944.
74. *Catholic Exponent*, August 13, 1993.
75. *Youngstown Vindicator*, April 14, 1935.
76. *Catholic Exponent*, August 13, 1993.
77. McDermott, interview.
78. *Catholic Exponent*, August 13, 1993.
79. McDermott, interview.
80. *Youngstown Vindicator*, April 4–5, 1964.
81. *Youngstown Vindicator*, May 5, 1944.
82. *Youngstown Vindicator*, April 4–5, 1964.
83. *Youngstown Vindicator*, May 5, 1944.
84. Meshel, interview.
85. *Youngstown Vindicator*, April 4–5, 1964.
86. *Youngstown Vindicator*, May 5, 1944.
87. *Youngstown Vindicator*, April 4–5, 1964.
88. *Youngstown Vindicator*, May 25, 1945.

Chapter 3

89. *Youngstown Vindicator*, August 15, 1945.

90. *Ursulinian* (1950).

91. Mulqueen, interview.

92. Lynch and Dean, "Where We've Been," 14.

93. *Ursuline High School Jubilee, 1905–1980.*

94. Lynch and Dean, "Where We've Been," 14.

95. Rudge, interviews.

96. Lynch and Dean, "Where We've Been," 24–26.

97. Rudge, interviews.

98. *Youngstown Vindicator*, April 4–5, 1964.

99. *Youngstown Vindicator*, August 1, 1954.

100. Gillon, *American Paradox*, 86.

101. *Youngstown Vindicator*, June 7, 1955.

102. Clarke, interview.

103. *Youngstown Vindicator*, September 29, 1957.

104. *Youngstown Vindicator*, September 16, 1955.

105. *Youngstown Vindicator*, January 13, 1967.

106. Gabert, *In Hoc Signo?*, 94.

107. *Catholic Exponent*, May 7, 1993.

108. Jenkins, *Steel Valley Klan*, 19–22.

109. *Youngstown Vindicator*, September 3, 1954.

110. Kolp, interview.

111. *Youngstown Vindicator*, September 3, 1954.

112. Ibid.

113. Rudge, interviews.

114. "Cathedral Parish of St. Columba," 11.

115. *Youngstown Vindicator*, November 10, 1958.

116. Morris, *American Catholic*, 281.

117. Dawson, interview.

Chapter 4

118. Appleby, Byrne and Portier, *Creative Fidelity*, 285.

119. McGreevey, *Catholicism and American Freedom*, 237.

120. Hennesey, *American Catholics*, 309.

121. Dolan, *In Search of an American Catholicism*, 192.

122. *Youngstown Vindicator*, October 10, 1960.
123. Fuechtmann, *Steeples and Stacks*, 29.
124. McNicholas, interviews.
125. Lynch and Dean, "Where We've Been," 29–30.
126. Ibid., 31.
127. Ibid., 30–31.
128. *Youngstown Vindicator*, May 25, 1961.
129. Lynch and Dean, "Where We've Been," 31.
130. McNicholas, interviews.
131. Lynch and Dean, "Where We've Been," 30–31.
132. *Youngstown Vindicator*, May 18, 1965.
133. *Youngstown Vindicator*, May 10, 1964.
134. *Youngstown Vindicator*, May 25, 1964.
135. Lynch and Dean, "Where We've Been," 32.
136. Ibid., 33–34.
137. O'Neill, interview.
138. Cummings, interview.
139. Lynch and Dean, "Where We've Been," 35–39.
140. Ibid., 2.
141. Ibid., 25.
142. Ibid., 15.
143. Ibid., 40–41.
144. Ibid., 38–39.
145. Ibid., 41–42.
146. *Youngstown Vindicator*, March 30, 1963.
147. Lynch and Dean, "Where We've Been," 41–42.
148. Raupple, interview.
149. Rogers, interview.
150. Buetow, *Of Singular Benefit*, 302–3.
151. Briggs, *Double Crossed*, 121.
152. Ibid., 117.
153. Lynch and Dean, "Where We've Been," 44–45.
154. Baluch, interview.
155. Ulicney, interview.
156. Ibid.
157. Murphy, interview.
158. Ibid.
159. Rudge, interviews.
160. Massa, *Catholics and American Culture*, 155.

161. O'Donnell, *Playing with Fire*, 44.

162. Buetow, *Of Singular Benefit*, 319–20.

163. Steinfels, *A People Adrift*, 257.

164. *Youngstown Vindicator*, November 29, 1981.

165. Carney, interview.

166. *Youngstown Vindicator*, January 13, 1967.

167. *Youngstown Vindicator*, August 5, 1969.

168. *Catholic Exponent*, August 13, 1993.

Chapter 5

169. *Catholic Exponent*, August 13, 1993.

170. *Youngstown Vindicator*, November 17, 1976.

171. Winsen, interview.

172. "Internal Records for Immaculate Conception School."

173. *Youngstown Vindicator*, June 13, 1969.

174. "Internal Records for Immaculate Conception School."

175. Italiano, interview.

176. Briggs. *Double Crossed*, 52–53.

177. *Youngstown Vindicator*, November 16, 1970.

178. Winsen, interview.

179. *Youngstown Vindicator*, February 12, 1970.

180. Winsen, interview.

181. Vogelsang, interview.

182. Linkon and Russo, *Steeltown U.S.A.*, 43–44.

183. *Youngstown Vindicator*, September 3, 1972.

184. Iskander, interview.

185. *Youngstown Vindicator*, November 24, 1974.

186. *Centennial of Service*.

187. Vogelsang, interview.

188. Koval, interview.

189. Lynch and Dean, "Where We've Been," 53–54.

190. Ibid., 64.

191. Rudge, interviews.

192. Lynch and Dean, "Where We've Been," 84–85.

193. Ibid., 87–88.

194. Rudge, interviews.

195. Fuechtmann, *Steeples and Stacks*, 1.

196. *Wall Street Journal*, September 23, 1980.
197. Bruno, *Steelworker Alley*, 149.

Chapter 6

198. Fuechtmann, *Steeples and Stacks*, 4–5.
199. *New York Times*, November 19, 1983.
200. Greeley, *Making of the Pope*, 115.
201. Bernstein and Politi, *His Holiness*, 11–13.
202. Ibid., 462.
203. Ibid., 429.
204. Steinfels, *A People Adrift*, 35.
205. Welsh, interview.
206. *Youngstown Vindicator*, June 23, 1984.
207. Welsh, interview.
208. Lynch and Dean, "Where We've Been," 106.
209. Welsh, interview.
210. *Youngstown Vindicator*, April 5, 1986.
211. Ibid.
212. Kennedy, interview.
213. *Youngstown Vindicator*, February 1, 1988.
214. Fleming, interview.
215. Rogers, interview.
216. *Youngstown Vindicator*, August 11, 1984.
217. *Youngstown Vindicator*, June 23, 1985.
218. Bryk, Lee and Holland, *Catholic Schools and the Common Good*, 52.
219. *Youngstown Vindicator*, April 3, 1977.
220. *Youngstown Vindicator*, August 2, 1985.
221. *Youngstown Vindicator*, December 22, 1986.
222. York, interview.
223. Scarsella, interview.
224. *Youngstown Vindicator*, October 21, 1985.
225. *Youngstown Vindicator*, October 11, 1986.
226. Dawson, interview.
227. Ricciuti, interview.
228. *Youngstown Vindicator*, April 29, 1989.
229. *Youngstown Vindicator*, December 10, 1988.

Chapter 7

230. *Youngstown Vindicator*, February 11, 1990.
231. McNicholas, interviews.
232. Rudge, interviews.
233. *Youngstown Vindicator*, May 22, 1993.
234. Critell, interview.
235. *Youngstown Vindicator*, May 22, 1993.
236. "Ursuline Center."
237. *Youngstown Vindicator*, December 12, 1994.
238. McNicholas, interviews.
239. *Metro Eye*, July 1994.
240. McNicholas, interviews.
241. *Metro Eye*, July 1994.
242. Ibid.
243. McNicholas, interviews.
244. *Metro Eye*, July 1994.
245. McNicholas, interviews.
246. *Metro Eye*, July 1994.
247. *Youngstown Vindicator*, February 24, 1997.
248. *Youngstown Vindicator*, March 12, 1997.
249. *Youngstown Vindicator*, July 1, 1999.
250. McNicholas, interviews.
251. *Youngstown Vindicator*, June 27, 1994.
252. Lynch and Dean, "Where We've Been," 67.
253. Minchin, interview.
254. Kennedy, interview.
255. *Youngstown Vindicator*, August 26, 1991.
256. *Youngstown Vindicator*, January 2, 1992.
257. *Youngstown Vindicator*, April 7, 1992.
258. *Youngstown Vindicator*, February 12, 1995.
259. *Youngstown Vindicator*, March 16, 1995.
260. Lynch and Dean, "Where We've Been," 97.
261. Rudge, interviews.
262. LoGrasso, interview.
263. Toth, interview.
264. LoGrasso, interview.
265. Toth, interview.
266. "Missionary Service to Latin America."

267. Kundracik, interview.

268. Lynch and Dean, "Where We've Been," 92.

269. Kundracik, interview.

270. Lynch and Dean, "Where We've Been," 92–93.

271. Kundracik, interview.

272. Lynch and Dean, "Where We've Been," 93.

273. Kundracik, interview.

274. Raupple, interview.

275. Lynch and Dean, "Where We've Been," 76.

276. Raupple, interview.

Chapter 8

277. *Youngstown Vindicator*, June 7, 2006.

278. Italiano, interview.

279. *Youngstown Vindicator*, June 7, 2006.

280. Triplett, interview.

281. *Catholic Exponent*, September 9, 1994.

282. "Announcement of Ursuline Associates Program."

283. Assion, interview.

284. Ray Novotny, interview.

285. Eileen Walsh Novotny, interview.

286. Ray Novotny, interview.

287. Peggy Eicher, interview.

288. Dan Eicher, interview.

289. Peggy Eicher, interview.

290. *Youngstown Vindicator*, July 15, 2013.

291. Linda McClure, interview.

292. Larry McClure, interview.

293. Wakefield, interview.

294. Ricciuti, interview.

295. "Ursuline Sisters Senior Living."

296. "Open House Announced."

297. BSHM Architects Inc., "Ursuline Motherhouse Renovations, Canfield, Ohio."

298. Peggy Eicher, interview.

299. Arditi, interview.

300. Raupple, interview.

301. *Voices from Angela's Villa.*
302. Schulick, interview.
303. Wakefield, interview.
304. *Business Journal,* November 8, 2017.
305. Kennedy, interview.
306. McCormick, interview.
307. Kennedy, interview.
308. "Growth Report 1," *Business Journal,* 2022.
309. *Business Journal,* February 6, 2023.
310. *Youngstown Vindicator,* January 7, 2023.
311. Ulicney, interview.
312. Schulick, interview.
313. Murphy, interview.
314. Clarke, interview.
315. Noga, interview.
316. H. William Lawson, interview.
317. Joan Reedy Lawson, interview.
318. McCormick, interview.
319. Kennedy, interview.
320. Bonnot, interview.
321. McCormick, interview.

BIBLIOGRAPHY

Books

Appleby, R. Scott, Patricia Byrne and William L. Portier, eds. *Creative Fidelity: American Catholic Intellectual Traditions*. New York: Orbis Books, 2004.

Bernstein, Carl, and Marco Politi. *His Holiness: John Paul II and the History of Our Time*. New York: Penguin Books, 1996.

Blue, Frederick J., William D. Jenkins, H. William Lawson and Joan M. Reedy. *Mahoning Memories: A History of Youngstown and Mahoning County*. Virginia Beach, VA: Donning, 1995.

Briggs, Kenneth. *Double Crossed: Uncovering the Catholic Church's Betrayal of American Nuns*. New York: Doubleday, 2006.

Bruno, Robert. *Steelworker Alley: How Class Works in Youngstown*. Ithaca, NY: Cornell University Press, 1999.

Bryk, Anthony S., Valerie E. Lee and Peter B. Holland. *Catholic Schools and the Common Good*. Cambridge, MA: Harvard University Press, 1993.

Buetow, Harold A. *Of Singular Benefit: The Story of Catholic Education in the United States*. New York: MacMillan, 1970.

Buser, Sister Martha, OSU. *Also in Your Midst: Reflections on the Spirituality of St. Angela Merici*. St. Meinrad, IN: Abbey Press, 1990.

Dolan, Jay P. *In Search of an American Catholicism: A History of Religion and Culture in Tension*. New York: Oxford University Press, 2003.

Fuechtmann, Thomas G. *Steeples and Stacks: Religion and Steel Crisis in Youngstown*. Cambridge, UK: Cambridge University Press, 1989.

Gabert, Glen, Jr. *In Hoc Signo? A Brief History of Catholic Parochial Education in America.* Port Washington, NY: Kennikat Press, 1972.

Gillon, Steven M. *The American Paradox: A History of the United States Since 1945.* Boston, MA: Houghton Mifflin Company, 2003.

Greeley, Andrew M. *The Making of the Pope 2005.* New York: Little, Brown and Company, 2005.

Gross, Michael B. *The War Against Catholicism: Liberalism and the Anti-Catholic Imagination in Nineteenth Century Germany.* Ann Arbor: Michigan University Press, 2005.

Hennesey, James. *American Catholics: A History of the Roman Catholic Church in the United States.* New York: Oxford University Press, 1981.

Jenkins, William D. *Steel Valley Klan: The Ku Klux Klan in Ohio's Mahoning Valley.* Kent, OH: Kent State University Press, 1990.

Ledochowska, Teresa, OSU. *Angela Merici and the Company of St. Ursula.* Vol. 1. Rome: Ancora, 1969.

Linkon, Sherry, and John Russo. *Steeltown U.S.A.: Work and Memory in Youngstown.* Lawrence: University of Kansas, 2002.

Mahoney, Lelia, Sr., OSU. *A Tree in the Valley: The Highlights of the Annals of the Ursuline Convent of the Sacred Heart, Toledo, Ohio, 1854–1879.* Toledo, OH: Ursuline Sisters of Toledo, 1979.

Massa, Mark S. *Catholics and American Culture: Fulton Sheen, Dorothy Day, and the Notre Dame Football Team.* New York: Herder & Herder, 2001.

McFadden, James A. *The March of the Eucharist from Dungannon.* Youngstown, OH: Diocese of Youngstown, 1951.

McGreevey, John T. *Catholicism and American Freedom: A History.* New York: W.W. Norton & Co., 2004.

Morris, Charles R. *American Catholic: The Saints and Sinners Who Built America's Most Powerful Church.* New York: Vintage, 1997.

O'Donnell, Lawrence. *Playing with Fire: The 1968 Election and the Transformation of American Politics.* New York: Penguin Books, 2017.

Steinfels, Peter. *A People Adrift: The Crisis of the Roman Catholic Church in America.* New York: Simon & Schuster, 2003.

Journal Articles

Leonard, Henry B. "Ethnic Tensions, Episcopal Leadership and the Emergence of the Twentieth-Century American Catholic Church: The Cleveland Experience." *Catholic Historical Review* 71, no. 3 (July 1985): 394–412.

Interviews

Arditi, Bonnie Lynn. Interview by Thomas Welsh. September 6, 2022.

Assion, Mary Yvo. Interview by Thomas Welsh. September 28, 2022.

Bonnot, Father Robert. Interview by Thomas Welsh. October 13, 2022.

Carney, Mary Rita (McNicholas). Interview by Thomas Welsh. August 31, 2022.

Clarke, Monsignor James "Jay." Interview by Thomas Welsh. October 18, 2022.

Critell, Mary Ann. Interview by Michele Ristich Gatts. May 15, 2023.

Cummings, Jim. Interview by Thomas Welsh. December 19, 2022.

Dawson, Sister Nancy, OSU. Interview by Thomas Welsh. August 9, 2023.

Eicher, Dan. Interview by Thomas Welsh. October 10, 2022.

Eicher, Peggy. Interview by Thomas Welsh. October 10, 2022.

Fleming, Patricia McCabe. Interview by Thomas Welsh. October 14, 2022.

Iskander, Sister Marie Madeleine, R.A. Interview by Thomas Welsh. October 3, 2022.

Italiano, Sister Charlotte, OSU. Interview by Thomas Welsh. September 15, 2022.

Kennedy, Brigid. Interview by Thomas Welsh. October 12, 2023.

Kolp, Monsignor James. Interview by Thomas Welsh. September 25, 2022.

Koval, Sister Mary Alyce, OSU. Interview by Thomas Welsh. August 18, 2022.

Kundracik, Sister Dorothy, OSU. Interview by Michele Ristich Gatts. May 11, 2023.

Lawson, H. William. Interview by Thomas Welsh. October 24, 2022.

Lawson, Joan Reedy. Interview by Thomas Welsh. October 24, 2022.

LoGrasso, Sister Marlene, OSU. Interview by Thomas Welsh. June 7, 2023.

McClure, Larry. Interview by Thomas Welsh. July 14, 2023.

McClure, Linda. Interview by Thomas Welsh. July 14, 2023.

McCormick, Sister Mary, OSU. Interview by Thomas Welsh. June 15, 2023.

McNicholas, Sister Patricia, OSU. Interviews by Thomas Welsh. April 4, 2022; September 9, 2022.

Meshel, Harry. Interview by Thomas Welsh. September 16, 2013.

Minchin, Sister Kathleen, OSU. Interview by Thomas Welsh. September 8, 2022.

Mulqueen, Father John. Interview by Thomas Welsh. September 12, 2022.

Murphy, Father Richard. Interview by Thomas Welsh. September 19, 2022.

Novotny, Eileen Walsh. Interview by Thomas Welsh. September 20, 2022.

Novotny, Ray. Interview by Thomas Welsh. September 20, 2022.

O'Neill, Ed. Interview by Thomas Welsh. December 19, 2022.

Raupple, Sister Norma, OSU. Interview by Thomas Welsh. August 19, 2022.

Ricciuti, Paul. Interview by Thomas Welsh. August 29, 2022.

Rogers, Sister Regina, OSU. Interview by Thomas Welsh. August 16, 2022.

Rudge, Sister Isabel, OSU. Interviews by Thomas Welsh. March 9, 2022; July 28, 2022.

Scarsella, Richard S. Interview by Thomas Welsh. August 20, 2022.

Schulick, Scott. Interview by Thomas Welsh. October 5, 2022.

Toth, Sister Diane, OSU. Interview by Thomas Welsh. June 7, 2023.

Triplett, Shelia. Interview by Thomas Welsh. September 26, 2023.

Ulicney, John. Interview by Thomas Welsh. August 9, 2022.

Vogelsang, Sister Darla Jean, OSU. Interview by Thomas Welsh. September 20, 2022.

Wakefield, Dan. Interview by Thomas Welsh. July 17, 2023.

York, Denise DeBartolo. Interview by Thomas Welsh. August 9, 2022.

Documents and Memos

"Announcement of Ursuline Associates Program, September 2002." Memo. Ursuline Sisters of Youngstown Archives. Canfield, OH.

"Internal Records for Immaculate Conception School, 1969–1970." St. Angela Merici Parish Archives. Youngstown, OH.

"Missionary Service to Latin America." Document. Ursuline Sisters of Youngstown. Youngstown, OH.

"Youngstown Ursulines: Significant Dates." Document. Ursuline Sisters of Youngstown Archives. Canfield, OH.

Newspapers and Periodicals

Business Journal (2017)

Catholic Exponent (1993)

Cleveland Plain Dealer (1974)

High Gear (1958)

Liberty News (1974)

Metro Eye (1994)

New York Times
Wall Street Journal (1980)
Youngstown Telegram (1919–30).
Youngstown (OH) *Vindicator* (1895–2023)

Oral Histories

Baluch, Sister Julia, OSU. Interview by Thomas Welsh. April 24, 2007. Transcript 314. Mahoning Valley Historical Society. Youngstown, OH.
Italiano, Sister Charlotte, OSU. Interview by Thomas Welsh. May 31, 2007. Transcript 314. Mahoning Valley Historical Society. Youngstown, OH.
McDermott, Sister Virginia, OSU. Interview by Thomas Welsh. May 31, 2007. Transcript 314. Mahoning Valley Historical Society. Youngstown, OH.
Welsh, Sister Marcia, OSU. Interview by Thomas Welsh. January 23, 2003. Transcript 314. Mahoning Valley Historical Society. Youngstown, OH.
Winsen, Sister Teresa, OSU. Interview by Thomas Welsh. January 30, 2007. Transcript 314. Mahoning Valley Historical Society. Youngstown, OH.

Pamphlets and Programs

"The Cathedral Parish of St. Columba, Youngstown, Ohio, 150 Years of Faith, 1847–1997." Program. Youngstown, OH: Mahoning Valley Historical Society.
Centennial of Service: Ursuline Nuns of Youngstown. Canfield, OH: Ursuline Sisters of Youngstown, 1974.
"Entertainment for the Benefit of Ursuline Sisters at the Catholic Schoolhouse (Corner Rayen Avenue and Elm Street), Wednesday Evening, April 7th." Program. Canfield, OH: Ursuline Sisters of Youngstown.
"The New Ursuline High School, 751 Bryson Street, Youngstown, Ohio." Program. Canfield, OH: Ursuline Sisters of Youngstown.
"The Seventy-Fifth Anniversary of St. Ann's Church, October 29, 1944." Program. Youngstown, OH: Mahoning Valley Historical Society.
"The Ursuline Center: Ritual of Dedication." Program. Canfield, OH: Ursuline Sisters of Youngstown, August 29, 1993.
Ursuline High School Jubilee, 1905–1980. Youngstown, OH: Ursuline High School, 1980.

Unpublished Texts

Lynch, Sister Anne, OSU, and Sister Mary Allen Dean, OSU. "Where
We've Been…Where We're Going: A History of the Ursuline Sisters of
Youngstown." Unpublished manuscript. Canfield, OH: Ursuline Sisters
of Youngstown.

Websites

BSHM Architects Inc. "Ursuline Motherhouse Renovations, Canfield, Ohio."
https://www.bshm-architects.com/project/ursuline-motherhouse-
renovations/.
Rich, Sister Therese Ann. "Open House Announced for Ursuline Sisters
Senior Living." Ursuline Sisters of Youngstown, Ohio. September 4, 2013.
https://www.theursulines.org/2013/09/04/open-house-announced-for-
ursuline-sisters-senior-living/.
———. "Ursuline Sisters Senior Living." Ursuline Sisters of Youngstown,
Ohio. October 6, 2012. https://www.theursulines.org/2012/10/06/
ursuline-sisters-senior-living/.
Voices from Angela's Villa. http://voicesfromangelasvilla.weebly.com/our-
story.html.

Yearbooks

Ursulinian. Youngstown, OH: Ursuline High School, 1950.
Ursulinian. Youngstown, OH: Ursuline High School, 1964.

INDEX

ABOUT THE AUTHOR

 Thomas Welsh is a professional writer based in Youngstown, Ohio. He is the author of *Closing Chapters: Urban Change, Religious Reform, and the Decline of Youngstown's Catholic Elementary Schools* (Lexington Books, 2011). Since earning his doctorate at Kent State University, he has coauthored three books: *Strouss': Youngstown's Dependable Store* (The History Press, 2012), *Classic Restaurants of Youngstown* (The History Press, 2014) and *A History of Jewish Youngstown and the Steel Valley* (The History Press, 2017). He currently serves as an adjunct faculty member at Youngstown State University.

Visit us at
www.historypress.com